ROOTED

VOLUME ONE

Treehouse Schoolhouse

Treehouse Schoolhouse Press

ROOTED FAMILY BIBLE CURRICULUM, VOLUME ONE

Scripture quotations are from The ESV® Bible (The Holy Bible, English Standard Version®), copyright © 2001 by Crossway, a publishing ministry of Good News Publishers. Used by permission. All rights reserved.

Copyright © 2023, Treehouse Schoolhouse Press.

ISBN: 979-8-218-25290-8

Text by Lyndsey Mimnagh
Book design by Gabrielle Jones
Illustrated by Molly Van Roekel

All rights reserved. No part of this publication may be reproduced, distributed, or transmitted in any form or by any means including copying, recording, or other electronic or mechanical methods without the prior written permission of the publisher.

Printed in the United States of America

Treehouse Schoolhouse has been empowering families to educate and disciple children since 2017. Our home education tools and curriculum are now used by families all over the world. For more information, please email contact@treehouseschoolhouse.com or visit our website at www.treehouseschoolhouse.com.

CONTENTS

Introduction 4

Note from the Author 7

Resources 8

IDENTITY

Week 1: *I was created with a purpose* 9

Week 2: *I am deeply loved by God* 19

Week 3: *I am forgiven and free from sin* 29

Week 4: *I am adopted into God's family* 39

Week 5: *I am God's friend* 49

Week 6: *I was made to worship* 59

DEVOTION

Week 7: *I will love the Lord with all my heart, soul, mind, and strength* 69

Week 8: *I will seek first the kingdom of God in all I do* 79

Week 9: *I will trust God in good times and bad.* 89

Week 10: *I will read and study God's word* 99

Week 11: *I will talk to God and He talks to me* 109

Week 12: *I will trust God, even when I don't understand* 119

WISDOM

Week 13: *I will walk on the path of life* 129

Week 14: *I will honor my parents and authorities* 139

Week 15: *I will take my thoughts captive and think on true things* 149

Week 16: *I will accept correction and guidance with humility* 159

Week 17: *I will be a good steward of all that I have* 169

Week 18: *I will resist temptation and say no to sin* 179

INTRODUCTION

Rooted is an invitation to gather your family and dig deep into the rich soil of God's Word—together. It is a tool to instill courage, confidence, and Biblical character in your children by rooting them in their heavenly identity, the wisdom of scripture, and a lasting family culture of chasing after God's heart. From a position of being grounded, you will go on a mission together to discover God's plan for you on this earth.

Each week your family will learn declarations of truth about who you are created to be and how you will influence the world for the kingdom of God. Children will be inspired to rise up against the culture and be set apart in character and actions in our ever-changing world.

Overview of *Rooted, Volume One*

Rooted, Volume One focuses on growing deep roots of identity in Christ, a devoted heart, and a life of wisdom. The hope is that when we instill these truths in our children when they are young, their roots will grow deep and strong and they will be able to weather the storms and changes of life when they are adults.

Each week focuses on one facet of a rooted identity in Christ, devotion to God, and wisdom from God. All of the elements of the lessons throughout the week reinforce that truth.

Here is an overview of each section of the daily plans:

Declare — Lead your children to say the week's declaration statement three times. As you go through the study, say all of the declaration statements you have learned so far, in order. This simple daily act will help your children memorize these declarations and get them deep into their hearts.

Sing — Click on the link to Spotify each day and sing along to the hymn or worship song with your children. The lyrics are provided at the beginning of each section, as well as in the display sheets. Take it a step further and use instruments, as well as discussing the lyrics and meanings with your children.

Read — You will read a portion of scripture and a short paragraph summarizing the main ideas in the reading. I recommend asking your children to also locate the passages in their Bibles and read along. After you read, encourage your children to orally narrate what you read.

Discuss Each day has a few discussion question prompts for you to get the conversation going. Let this be a starting point for your family to meditate on the truths of God's Word together.

A note about narration: In a nutshell, narration is "the art of telling back" what the child has read or heard. It is a method that strengthens the student's habit of attention and secures the information in the mind. It is a skill that requires attention and more mental energy than you may think. If your children are new to narration, you can expect it to be a challenge for them. Give them something to play with like modeling clay or legos while you read. This will help their mind engage. When you finish, ask them to tell you the main points of what you read. Break the passages into small chunks and pause to narrate between readings if needed.

Beauty The beauty section is when you will engage with poetry and art. Each day there is a simple way for you to interact with the pieces, such as playing *Hide & Describe*, learning new vocabulary, using a prompt question to get the discussion going, and copying a selection of the work. On Fridays, you will invite your child to illustrate the poem or the art piece.

How to play Hide & Describe: Have the children study the piece of art for a few minutes, encouraging them to pay attention to the details. Tell them to take a picture of it in their mind. Turn the picture over and ask them to describe it. See how many details they can remember. If you are doing this with many children, start with the youngest first.

Recite Your family will memorize one passage of scripture each week by reciting it daily. At the beginning of the week, allow your children to read it. Toward the end, ask them to try to say it without looking. Use this time to also review past weeks' verses.

Pray Each day we offer prayer prompts to get your family started, but you should use it as a launching board to share what is on your heart. Model prayer to your children and encourage them to pray aloud as well. Over time, you will see the fruit of this practice and will be thankful for the beginnings and baby steps!

Connection Activities

The section at the bottom of each day is an optional activity for you to reinforce the day's lesson in a fun, hands-on way. These activities are perfect for homeschool families, as a way to connect the Bible lesson to other subjects like geography, writing, and math. In this section, you will find activities such as role-play, serving opportunities, and more Bible research and study. Often your child will have a prompt to write and draw in their Bible Notebook.

Schedule Ideas for Using *Rooted*

Regardless of your family's schedule, you can find a way to prioritize gathering together to study God's Word together. Do not feel like you need to use all of the study to be effective. Use *Rooted* as a menu and let it serve your family by using which elements work best for you. Here are some ideas:

- Complete the day's lesson over breakfast each morning. Giving children something to eat or play with quietly with their hands often helps them listen.

- Split the day's lesson into pieces. Do some together in the morning, and then add in any pieces of the study that include writing, drawing, and the Connection Activity after your child gets home from school or during your homeschool lessons later in the day.

- Use *Rooted* in the evenings, after dinner as a family devotional.

- Spread one week into two weeks if you have trouble fitting it in each weekday.

Materials

Rooted was designed to be open-and-go which means the materials you will need are simple and likely what you already have in your home.

- Bible - I recommend everyone in the family have a Bible to look up passages and take turns reading them aloud. The scripture passage display sheets are in ESV. However, you are welcome to use any version of the Bible to read from and memorize scripture.

- Bible Notebook - Each child should have a Bible Notebook. This can be any blank-page notebook or sketchbook. We have also provided *Rooted Bible Notebook* lined pages with blank space for illustrating in the digital files. You can print either primary lines or intermediate, depending on the level of your child. I recommend sliding the cover page in the front of a 3-ring binder and hole-punching the sheets to put inside.

- Lined paper - Each week your child will copy the week's scripture and a part of the poem onto lined paper that is appropriate for their age. You could also place these sheets in their Bible Notebook.

- General school supplies - Some of the connection activities will call for general supplies such as scissors, markers, watercolor supplies, and colored pencils.

NOTE FROM THE AUTHOR

My heart in writing *Rooted* came from a desire to have a tool like this for our own discipleship journey with our children. I wanted something that could include all ages, but dove deep into the Word of God and didn't just scratch the surface. I desired a resource that would invite my children to fall in love with Jesus, while also teaching them practical wisdom for living life and instructing them in character training.

I have been diligent to be mindful of various Christian denominations as I have written *Rooted*, making it welcoming to everyone in the body of Christ. Even with my best efforts, I encourage you to read ahead and adjust your language if something does not align exactly with your theology.

Another point I would like to make is that often classical artwork depicting Jesus and other biblical scenes and people do not, unfortunately, show accurate skin tones. The goal of sharing art with children is to expose them to many artists' interpretations and expressions of biblical passages. I would encourage you to use this as an opportunity to continually discuss what the true nationalities of the people were in the art and what their skin tone would have been like. You may also find partially-clothed characters in the art selections. Please review the art and decide if you feel comfortable sharing it with your children before you begin each week.

Rooted uses the English Standard Version (ESV) because we feel this version is a great choice for personal reading, reflection and Scripture memorization. The ESV is known for its accurate faithfulness to the original text of the Bible combined with simplicity and beauty of expression. All direct quotations in *Rooted* are taken from the ESV. While the ESV does not capitalize pronouns that make reference to God, in texts outside of biblical quotations, we have chosen to capitalize pronouns referring to deity. We hope that using capitalization will help distinguish references to God or Jesus and improve clarity as you use this book.

It is my hope that this resource will be well-loved by your family and will be a tool to solidify your family's identity in Christ and for your home to become a launching pad for carriers of God's kingdom to the world.

Lyndsey Mimnagh

Lyndsey is a homeschool mama of four and the founder of Treehouse Schoolhouse. Before motherhood, Lyndsey had a career in children's ministry and special needs education. Her home education centers around living books and ideas, hands-on learning, nature exploration, and biblical discipleship. She shares experiences and home education inspiration as well as creates curriculum and resources for families around the world at www.treehouseschoolhouse.com.

RESOURCES

Throughout this study we recommend links to songs and videos that coordinate with the week's topic. For your convenience, links and QR codes are provided below. To scan the QR code, take a photo on your smartphone and follow the link provided.

Rooted, Volume One
YouTube Playlist

https://qrco.de/bduKNS

Rooted, Volume One
Spotify Playlist

https://qrco.de/bduKUt

Treehouse Schoolhouse
Website & Blog

www.treehouseschoolhouse.com

Identity:
I was created with a purpose.

Declaration: I was created with a purpose.

Hymn: "All Creatures of Our God and King"

Verse: Ephesians 2:10

Poem: "The Hand Divine" by Daniel C. Colesworthy

Artwork: *Garden of Eden* by Frederik Bouttats the Elder

For we are his workmanship, created in Christ Jesus for good works, which God prepared beforehand, that we should walk in them.

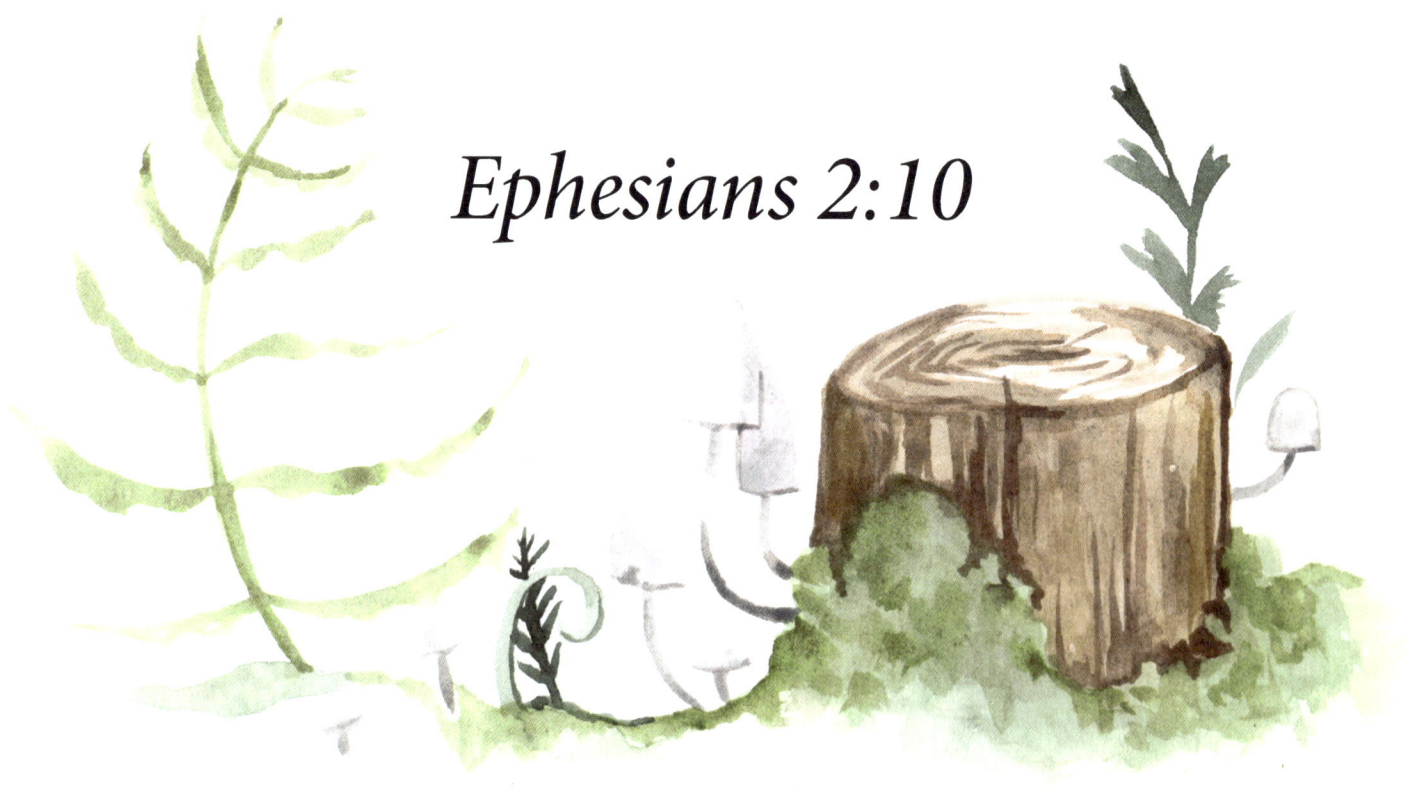

Ephesians 2:10

All Creatures of Our God and King

All creatures of our God and King
Lift up your voice and with us sing
Oh praise Him! Alleluia!
Thou burning sun with golden beam
Thou silver moon with softer gleam
Oh praise Him! (Oh praise Him!)
Alleluia! (Alleluia!) Alleluia!

Thou rushing wind that art so strong
Ye clouds that sail in heaven along
Oh praise Him! Alleluia!
Thou rising moon in praise rejoice
Ye light of evening find a voice
Oh praise Him! (Oh praise Him!)
Alleluia! (Alleluia!) Alleluia!

Let all things their Creator bless
And worship Him in humbleness
Oh praise Him! Alleluia!
Praise, praise the Father, praise the Son
And praise the Spirit three in one
Oh praise Him! (Oh praise Him!)
Alleluia! (Alleluia!) Alleluia!

The impress of a Hand Divine
On every thing I see:
The humblest flower, the tenderest vine,
Speak of a Deity.

There's not a plant that decks the spring,
A blossom, or a rose,
A blade of grass, an insect's wing,
But heavenly wisdom shows.

'Twas He who gave the lily birth,
And made the worlds on high;
In beauty spread the teeming earth
The God forever nigh.

'Tis everywhere I see and trace
The finger of his love;
Whose dwelling is unbounded space,
Around, below, above.

"The Hand Divine"
by Daniel C. Colesworthy

Identity: I was created with a purpose.

Garden of Eden by Frederik Bouttats the Elder
ca. 1611 and 1661

DAY 1

Declare Say "I was created with a purpose" three times.

Sing Sing the hymn "All Creatures of Our God and King" and follow along with the lyrics sheet.

Read Read Genesis 1:1-25.

Everything was created by God with a purpose. Even the smallest of creatures like worms and ants have an important role to play on the Earth.

Discuss What are your favorite things that God created?

Talk about how all things in nature point to God's creativity and power.

Beauty Observe *Garden of Eden* by Frederik Bouttats the Elder.
Play Hide & Describe.

Recite Recite Ephesians 2:10.

Pray Thank God for being the Creator of all things.

Ask God to help you remember Him when you are in nature and are delighting in the work of His hands.

Nature Study

Do some research in books or on the internet about the significance of worms or ants to the earth.

Write down what you learn and draw a picture to represent what you learned.

DAY 2

Declare   Say "I was created with a purpose" three times.

Sing   Sing the hymn "All Creatures of Our God and King" and follow along with the lyrics sheet.

Read   Read Genesis 1:26-31.

God created all things. While everything has a purpose, the most uniquely loved creations of God are people.

Discuss   What verses in the passage tell you that God views humans as the most important of His creation?

Do you ever feel insignificant? Why or why not?

How does it make you feel to know that the Creator of the universe looks at you and thinks that you are special?

Beauty   Read "The Hand Divine" by Daniel C. Colesworthy.
Discuss any unknown vocabulary and meanings.

Recite   Recite Ephesians 2:10.

Pray   Thank God for creating you as the most special of His creations.

Ask God to help you see yourself the way that He sees you.

Create

Draw or paint a self-portrait and write a list of things that you love about how God made you somewhere on the paper.

DAY 3

Declare Say "I was created with a purpose" three times.

Sing Sing the hymn "All Creatures of Our God and King" and follow along with the lyrics sheet.

Read Read Psalm 139:13-16.

Every person was intricately and intentionally created by God in their mother's womb. Before you were born, God had a purpose for your life and knew about each day you would live.

Discuss Read verse 14 again and then read these definitions translated from Hebrew:

- *Fearfully*: with great reverence and heart-felt interest
- *Wonderfully*: unique and set apart

What is something about you that makes you unique?

Beauty Observe *Garden of Eden* by Frederik Bouttats the Elder.
If you could walk into this picture, how would you feel and what would you do?

Recite Recite Ephesians 2:10.

Pray Thank God for creating all the details of your body.

Ask God to help you remember that you were made with a purpose.

Family Connection

Look at pictures together of you growing in your mother's body or as an infant.

Identity: I was created with a purpose.

DAY 4

Declare — Say "I was created with a purpose" three times.

Sing — Sing the hymn "All Creatures of Our God and King" and follow along with the lyrics sheet.

Read — Read Matthew 22:35-39.

One of the main purposes God created humans for is to show His love for us. God made us to demonstrate His love so that we can love Him back in return. Second in importance is to love our neighbor (everyone else)!

Discuss — What is one thing you can do this week to express your love to God?

What does it mean to love your neighbor as yourself?

Who is one person you will intentionally love this week? How will you do that?

Beauty — Read "The Hand Divine" by Daniel C. Colesworthy.
Recite any portions from memory or copy your favorite stanza.

Recite — Recite Ephesians 2:10.

Pray — Tell God you want to love Him with all your heart, soul, and mind.

Ask God to show you who in your life needs His love from you this week.

Dig Deeper

Talk about how all of God's commands are summed up in loving Him and loving others. Read Exodus 20:2-17 and discuss if each commandment is "covered" by loving God or loving others.

DAY 5

Declare Say "I was created with a purpose" three times.

Sing Sing the hymn "All Creatures of Our God and King" and follow along with the lyrics sheet.

Read Read Jeremiah 1:4-10.

Jeremiah had an important calling from God—to be a prophet. Before Jeremiah was born, God had assigned that mission to his life. When God told him, he felt unsure that he could speak and too young to fulfill the mission. God told Jeremiah not to be afraid and empowered him to do God's work.

Discuss Dream together about God's calling for you individually or collectively as a family.

Is there something you know God wants you to do but you are afraid?

What can you do when fear comes up in your heart when obeying God's call?

Beauty Replicate a portion or all of this week's artwork or draw or paint what you imagine when you read this week's poem.

Recite Recite Ephesians 2:10.

Pray Ask God to show you what your mission is individually and as a family.

Ask God to help you to be bold and brave in pursuing a life of service to Him.

Bible Notebook

Write a summary of the story you read today and draw a picture to represent it.

Identity:
I am deeply loved by God.

Declaration: I am deeply loved by God.

Hymn: "How Deep the Father's Love for Us"

Verse: 1 John 4:9

Poem: "Jesus Loves Me" by Anna Bartlett Warner

Artwork: *Suffer the Children* by Carl Heinrich Bloch

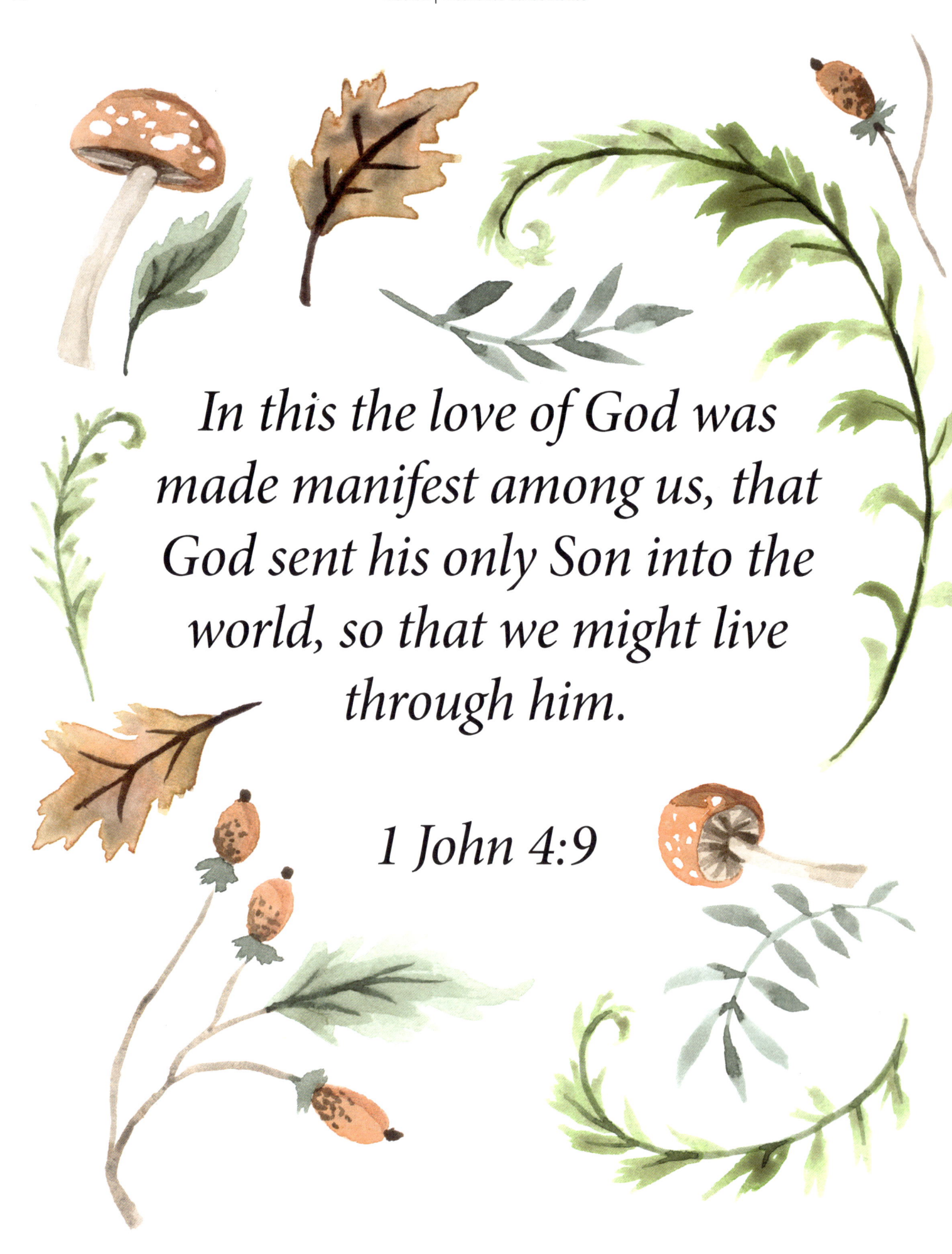

In this the love of God was made manifest among us, that God sent his only Son into the world, so that we might live through him.

1 John 4:9

How Deep the Father's Love for Us

How deep the Father's love for us
How vast beyond all measure
That He should give His only Son
To make a wretch His treasure

How great the pain of searing loss
The Father turns His face away
As wounds which mar the Chosen One
Bring many sons to glory

Behold the man upon a cross
My sin upon His shoulders
Ashamed, I hear my mocking voice
Call out among the scoffers

It was my sin that held Him there
Until it was accomplished
His dying breath has brought me life
I know that it is finished

I will not boast in anything
No gifts, no power, no wisdom
But I will boast in Jesus Christ
His death and resurrection

Why should I gain from His reward?
I cannot give an answer
But this I know with all my heart
His wounds have paid my ransom

Jesus loves me—this I know,
For the Bible tells me so:
Little ones to Him belong—
They are weak, but He is strong.

Jesus loves me—He who died
Heaven's gate to open wide;
He will wash away my sin,
Let His little child come in.

Jesus loves me—loves me still,
Though I'm very weak and ill;
From His shining throne on high,
Comes to watch me where I lie.

Jesus loves me—He will stay
Close beside me all the way.
Then His little child will take
Up to heaven for His dear sake.

"Jesus Loves Me"
by Anna Bartlett Warner

Identity: I am deeply loved by God.

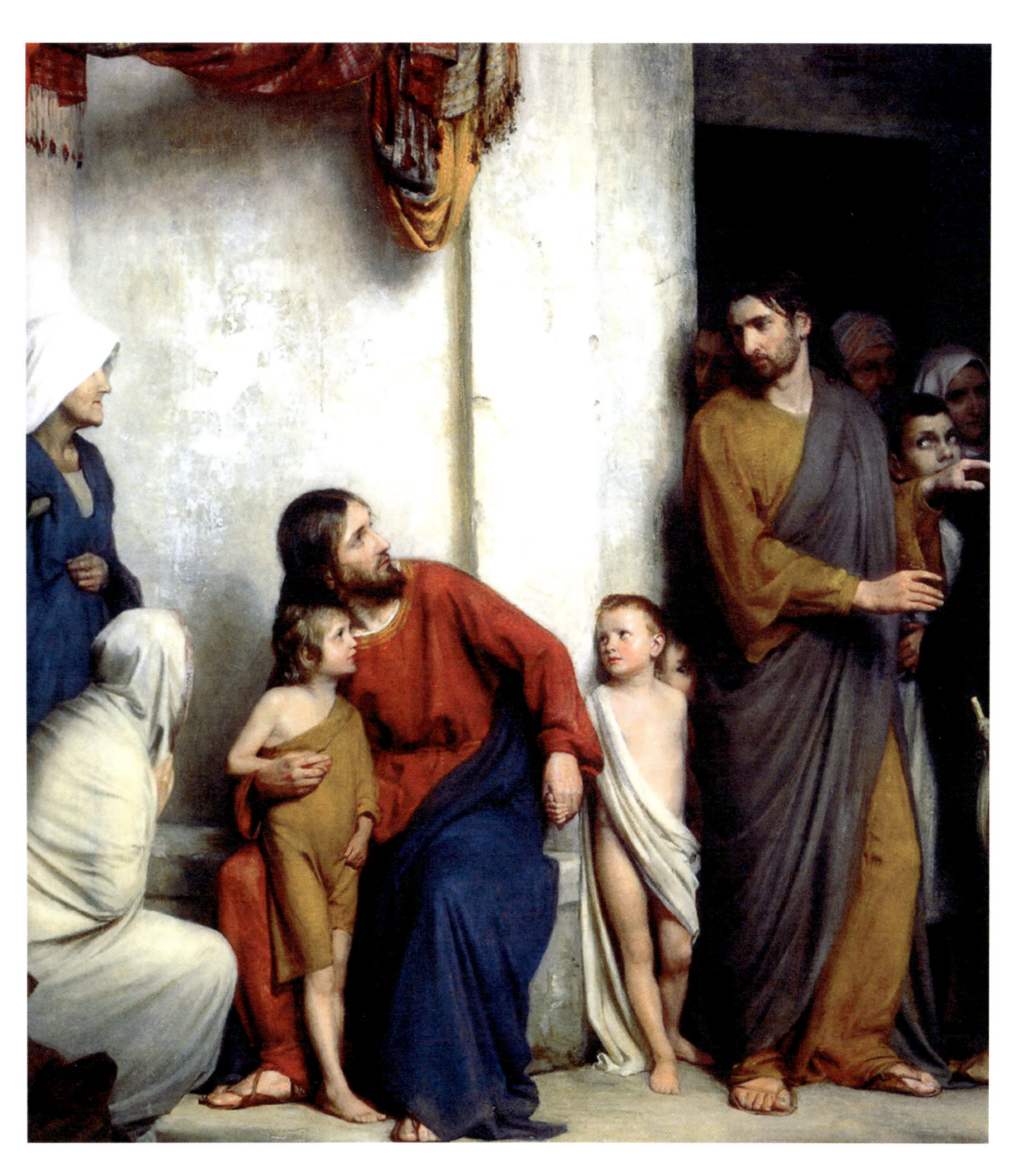

Suffer the Children by Carl Heinrich Bloch
ca. 1881

DAY 1

Declare   Say "I am deeply loved by God" three times.

Sing   Sing the hymn "How Deep the Father's Love for Us" and follow along with the lyrics sheet.

Read   Read John 19:16-37 and John 3:16.

The greatest act of love ever shown was when Jesus died on the cross. Jesus chose to die to pay the punishment for all of the sins in the world, including yours. Because He did that, you can have a relationship with God forever.

Discuss   Talk about a time that you felt so much love for someone that you would sacrifice something for their good.

Why did Jesus stay on the cross when he had the power to get off?

Beauty   Observe *Suffer the Children* by Carl Heinrich Bloch.
Play Hide & Describe.

Recite   Recite 1 John 4:9.

Pray   Thank God for choosing to die because of His great love for you, and tell God how much you love Him back.

Thank God for making a way for you to have a relationship with Him.

Create

Watercolor a picture of a heart or a cross. Cut out pictures of children from around the world in magazines or the internet and glue them around it. Copy John 3:16 somewhere on the paper.

Identity: I am deeply loved by God.

DAY 2

Declare   Say "I am deeply loved by God" three times.

Sing   Sing the hymn "How Deep the Father's Love for Us" and follow along with the lyrics sheet.

Read   Read Romans 5:8 and Ephesians 2:4-9.

God loved you before you were born. He loves you when you sin and when you behave well. His love isn't based on what you do or even if you love Him back. He offers us the free gift of salvation because of His love.

Discuss   Have you ever been given an undeserved gift? What did it feel like to receive it?

Talk about good works being a response to our love for God, rather than a means to earn salvation.

What does it mean in Ephesians 2:9 when it says, "so that no one may boast"?

Beauty   Read "Jesus Loves Me" by Anna Bartlett Warner.
Discuss any unknown vocabulary and meanings.

Recite   Recite 1 John 4:9.

Pray   Thank God for loving you before you chose Him and even when you sin.

Thank God for the free gift of salvation.

Confess any sin in your heart or life to God out of a response of love to Him.

History

Learn about the history of the poem and song "Jesus Loves Me" by watching the video. Scan the QR code in the introduction to watch it.

DAY 3

Declare — Say "I am deeply loved by God" three times.

Sing — Sing the hymn "How Deep the Father's Love for Us" and follow along with the lyrics sheet.

Read — Read Mark 10:13-16.

This happened during a time Jesus was teaching to a crowd. The disciples didn't think Jesus would want to be "bothered" by the little children, but Jesus didn't see them as a bother at all. He loved them and wanted them to come to Him.

Discuss — Have you ever had thoughts or feelings that the Bible and knowing God is an "adult thing"?

In verse 15, what does "enter the kingdom of God like a child" mean?

How does it make you feel that God doesn't view children as a bother?

Beauty — Observe *Suffer the Children* by Carl Heinrich Bloch. What do you think the children are thinking and feeling in this picture? What about Jesus?

Recite — Recite 1 John 4:9.

Pray — Thank God for loving children and especially for loving you!

Ask God to keep your heart soft towards Him and to always want to come to Him and learn from Him.

Bible Notebook

Write a summary of the story you read today and draw a picture to represent it.

Identity: I am deeply loved by God.

DAY 4

Declare   Say "I am deeply loved by God" three times.

Sing   Sing the hymn "How Deep the Father's Love for Us" and follow along with the lyrics sheet.

Read   Read Romans 8:31-39.

Paul was referencing the persecution that he and the church were facing. Even in the face of death, he knew God loved him. There is nothing powerful enough to separate you from God's love. Even when you go through hard times or you feel far from God, it's not because God stops loving you.

Discuss   Talk about a time you felt alone, afraid, or far from God. What did you do to overcome that?

In hard times, what can you do to help yourself remember that God is always with you and loves you?

Beauty   Read "Jesus Loves Me" by Anna Bartlett Warner.
Recite any portions from memory or copy your favorite stanza.

Recite   Recite 1 John 4:9.

Pray   Thank God for His strong love that never changes or leaves.

Tell God about any struggles you are having in feeling alone or far from Him.

Ask God to fill you with comfort and love.

Demonstrate

Mix two colors of paint or playdough together. Talk about how you can't separate the colors from each other once mixed, just like we can't be separated from God's love.

DAY 5

Declare   Say "I am deeply loved by God" three times.

Sing   Sing the hymn "How Deep the Father's Love for Us" and follow along with the lyrics sheet.

Read   Read Matthew 10:29-31 and Ephesians 3:16-19.

God loves and cares about the tiniest details of your life and even knows how many hairs you have on your head! Even something as insignificant as a sparrow matters to God. God's love is so great that we cannot fully measure or understand it.

Discuss   What is your most valued possession? How do you care for it?

Do you ever struggle to feel seen, known, and valuable to God?

How does it change the way you think and act when you begin to grasp God's love for you?

Beauty   Replicate a portion or all of this week's artwork or draw or paint what you imagine when you read this week's poem.

Recite   Recite 1 John 4:9.

Pray   Pray that your children would be rooted and established in God's love.

Thank God for his immeasurable love and for caring about the tiniest details in your life.

Math

Measure multiple items around the house with a tape measure. Go outside and ask your child to measure the sky. Talk about how it's impossible to do that, just as it's impossible to measure God's love for us.

Identity:
I am forgiven and free from sin.

Declaration: I am forgiven and free from sin.

Hymn: "Nothing but the Blood of Jesus"

Verse: Psalm 103:11-12

Poem: "Search Me, O God" by J. Edwin Orr

Artwork: *The Return of the Prodigal Son* by Bartolome Esteban Murillo

For as high as the heavens are above the earth, so great is his steadfast love toward those who fear him; as far as the east is from the west, so far does he remove our transgressions from us.

Psalm 103:11-12

Nothing But the Blood of Jesus

What can wash away my sin?
Nothing but the blood of Jesus
What can make me whole again?
Nothing but the blood of Jesus

O precious is the flow
That makes me white as snow
No other fount I know
Nothing but the blood of Jesus

For my pardon, this I see
Nothing but the blood of Jesus
For my cleansing, this my plea
Nothing but the blood of Jesus

O precious is the flow
That makes me white as snow
No other fount I know
Nothing but the blood of Jesus

Nothing can for sin atone
Nothing but the blood of Jesus
Naught of good that I have done
Nothing but the blood of Jesus

O precious is the flow
That makes me white as snow
No other fount I know
Nothing but the blood of Jesus

This is all my hope and peace
Nothing but the blood of Jesus
This is all my righteousness
Nothing but the blood of Jesus

O precious is the flow
That makes me white as snow
No other fount I know
Nothing but the blood of Jesus
(repeat)

Search me, O God, and know my heart today;
Try me, O Savior, know my thoughts, I pray.
See if there be some wicked way in me;
Cleanse me from every sin and set me free.

I praise Thee, Lord, for cleansing me from sin;
Fulfill Thy Word, and make me pure within.
Fill me with fire where once I burned with shame;
Grant my desire to magnify Thy Name.

Lord, take my life and make it wholly Thine;
Fill my poor heart with Thy great love divine.
Take all my will, my passion, self and pride;
I now surrender, Lord; in me abide.

O Holy Ghost, revival comes from Thee;
Send a revival, start the work in me.
Thy Word declares Thou wilt supply our need;
For blessings now, O Lord, I humbly plead.

"Search Me, O God"
by J. Edwin Orr

Identity: I am forgiven and free from sin.

The Return of the Prodigal Son by Bartolome Esteban Murillo
ca. 1881

DAY 1

Declare — Say "I am forgiven and free from sin" three times.

Sing — Sing the hymn "Nothing but the Blood of Jesus" and follow along with the lyrics sheet.

Read — Read Romans 3:23 and Romans 6:22-23.

Every person is born with a sinful nature and is in need of forgiveness from God. When you choose to follow Jesus, you exchange a life of slavery to sin for a life of freedom from sin and eternal life.

Discuss — Explain that the word "death" in the Bible often refers to spiritual death or separation from God.

Talk about what it means to be a "slave" to sin or to God.

Beauty — Observe *The Return of the Prodigal Son* by Bartolome Esteban Murillo. Play Hide & Describe.

Recite — Recite Psalm 103:11-12.

Pray — Confess that you know you are a sinner and need God's forgiveness.

Thank Jesus for making a way to be forgiven and free from slavery to sin.

Ask Jesus to forgive you for any sin in your heart or life.

Role Play

Have one child pretend they are trapped as a slave with no rights or freedoms. Have another child pretend to pay to set them free. How does the slave feel about the one who set them free? How does being free after being in slavery make them want to live their life?

Identity: I am forgiven and free from sin.

DAY 2

Declare   Say "I am forgiven and free from sin" three times.

Sing   Sing the hymn "Nothing but the Blood of Jesus" and follow along with the lyrics sheet.

Read   Read Hebrews 10:14-17 and Micah 7:18-19.

When God forgives us, it's as if He throws the sin into the deep sea and completely forgets it. He overlooks our sin and replaces it with His righteousness.

Discuss   Have you ever swam really deep into a pool, lake, or sea? Could you touch the bottom?

Discuss that God is omniscient (all-knowing), so while he *can* recall our sin, he views it as if it never happened.

Beauty   Read "Search Me, O God" by J. Edwin Orr.
Discuss any unknown vocabulary and meanings.

Recite   Recite Psalm 103:11-12.

Pray   Thank God for His deep love for you that causes Him to forgive your sin.

Tell God you love Him back and you want to obey His commands.

Bible Notebook / Geography

Do a study on the deepest body of water in the world, the Mariana Trench. Learn about how deep it is and locate it on a globe or map. Copy Micah 7:19 and draw a picture of a body of water. Write the words "my sins" at the bottom of the water.

DAY 3

Declare Say "I am forgiven and free from sin" three times.

Sing Sing the hymn "Nothing but the Blood of Jesus" and follow along with the lyrics sheet.

Read Read Luke 15:11-24.

The father in this parable represents God. Even when his son left and spent all of his inheritance, the father welcomed him back with open arms. God forgives and welcomes us back to him, no matter what we do.

Discuss What did the prodigal son expect his father to feel and do when he returned? What was the reality?

Did the prodigal son come with humility or pride? What does this show us about what the position of our hearts should be in repentance?

Beauty Observe *The Return of the Prodigal Son* by Bartolome Esteban Murillo. What emotions does this picture make you feel?

Recite Recite Psalm 103:11-12.

Pray Thank God for being a father to us and for being ready to forgive as soon as we "come home" to Him.

Ask Jesus to forgive you for any sin in your heart or life.

Bible Notebook

Write a summary of the story you read today and draw a picture to represent it.

DAY 4

Declare — Say "I am forgiven and free from sin" three times.

Sing — Sing the hymn "Nothing but the Blood of Jesus" and follow along with the lyrics sheet.

Read — Read Psalm 103.

This psalm is a song of praise. David was worshiping the Lord for many reasons in this song and the main one was for God's forgiveness. Our response to God's forgiveness should be praise and a life dedicated to Him.

Discuss — Read the psalm one more time and raise your hand every time you hear language about forgiveness.

How does receiving forgiveness cause a person to feel and act?

Beauty — Read "Search Me, O God" by J. Edwin Orr.
Recite any portions from memory or copy your favorite stanza.

Recite — Recite Psalm 103:11-12.

Pray — Write or sing your own psalm to God about how wonderful He is.

Ask God to help you always put your trust in Him.

Geography

Read or recite Psalm 103:12 again. Look at a picture of a compass and learn about cardinal directions. Go outside and explore using a real compass if you have one!

DAY 5

Declare — Say "I am forgiven and free from sin" three times.

Sing — Sing the hymn "Nothing but the Blood of Jesus" and follow along with the lyrics sheet.

Read — Read Ephesians 1:7 and Matthew 26:26-29.

Before Jesus left the earth, He gave His disciples bread and wine to symbolize His body and blood. Taking communion is a way we can pause and remember His sacrifice on the cross and His forgiveness of sins.

Discuss — Talk about the old covenant and how people had to shed animals' blood before Jesus came.

How does being forgiven by God make you want to respond to God and live your life?

Beauty — Replicate a portion or all of this week's artwork or draw or paint what you imagine when you read this week's poem.

Recite — Recite Psalm 103:11-12.

Pray — Thank Jesus for making the ultimate sacrifice and shedding His blood in order for us to be forgiven.

Ask God to help you be quick to forgive others as He has forgiven you.

Family Connection

Use grape juice and bread or crackers to take communion together as a family. As an alternative, draw a picture of bread and a glass of wine and copy Ephesians 1:7 in your Bible Notebook.

Identity:
I am adopted into God's family.

Declaration: I am adopted into God's family.

Song: "Good Good Father"

Verse: Romans 8:15

Poem: "Redeemed, How I Love to Proclaim It" by Fanny Cosby

Artwork: *Christ and the Children of All Races* by Vittorio Bianchini

For you did not receive the spirit of slavery to fall back into fear, but you have received the Spirit of adoption as sons, by whom we cry, "Abba! Father!"

Romans 8:15

Identity: I am adopted into God's family.

Good Good Father

Oh, I've heard a thousand stories of what they think You're like
But I've heard the tender whisper of love in the dead of night
And You tell me that You're pleased and that I'm never alone

You're a good, good Father
It's who You are, it's who You are, it's who You are
And I'm loved by You
It's who I am, it's who I am, it's who I am

Oh, and I've seen many searching for answers far and wide
But I know we're all searching for answers only You provide
'Cause You know just what we need before we say a word

You're a good, good Father
It's who You are, it's who You are, it's who You are
And I'm loved by You
It's who I am, it's who I am, it's who I am
Because You are perfect in all of Your ways
(repeat)

Oh, it's love so undeniable I, I can hardly speak
Peace so unexplainable I, I can hardly think

As You call me deeper still
As You call me deeper still
As You call me deeper still into love, love, love

You're a good, good Father
It's who You are, it's who You are, it's who You are
And I'm loved by You
It's who I am, it's who I am, it's who I am
(repeat)

You are perfect in all of your ways *(repeat)*

Redeemed, how I love to proclaim it!
Redeemed by the blood of the Lamb;
Redeemed through His infinite mercy,
His child and forever I am.

Redeemed, redeemed,
Redeemed by the blood of the Lamb;
Redeemed, redeemed,
His child and forever I am.

Redeemed, and so happy in Jesus,
No language my rapture can tell;
I know that the light of His presence
With me doth continually dwell.

I think of my blessed Redeemer,
I think of Him all the day long:
I sing, for I cannot be silent;
His love is the theme of my song.

I know there's a crown that is waiting,
In yonder bright mansion for me,
And soon, with the spirits made perfect,
At home with the Lord I shall be.

"Redeemed, How I Love to Proclaim It"
by Fanny Cosby

Identity: I am adopted into God's family.

Christ and the Children of All Races by Vittorio Bianchini
ca. 1797-1880

DAY 1

Declare Say "I am adopted into God's family" three times.

Sing Sing the song "Good Good Father" and follow along with the lyrics sheet.

Read Read Romans 8:12-15.

When we choose to follow Jesus, we are adopted into God's family! *Abba* is an Aramaic word that signifies the close, intimate relationship between a father and a child, similar to saying "Daddy."

Discuss Why is being a part of a family so important? What do you love about belonging to a family?

Talk about the differences between being a slave to a master and a child to a loving father.

Beauty Observe *Christ and the Children of All Races* by Vittorio Bianchini. Play Hide & Describe.

Recite Recite Romans 8:15.

Pray Ask God to help you not to be led by fear, but rather to be led by His Spirit in all you do.

Thank God for adopting you into His family.

Family Connection

If you know a family who has been blessed by adoption, reach out to ask if they can share their story with your family. Watch the testimony videos of adoption by scanning the QR in the introduction.

Identity: I am adopted into God's family.

DAY 2

Declare   Say "I am adopted into God's family" three times.

Sing   Sing the song "Good Good Father" and follow along with the lyrics sheet.

Read   Read Romans 8:16-17 and Ephesians 1:1-14.

An heir is someone who receives an inheritance, typically from an earthly father. As followers of Jesus, we are heirs of God! This means that we are entitled to receive everything our heavenly Father has promised.

Discuss   What do you receive every day because you are a child of your earthly parents? Do you have to beg or work for it?

What are the benefits of being adopted into God's family you heard in the reading?

Beauty   Read "Redeemed, How I Love to Proclaim It" by Fanny Cosby.
Discuss any unknown vocabulary and meanings.

Recite   Recite Romans 8:15.

Pray   Thank God for making you a joint heir with Christ and for all of His blessings and promises.

Ask God to help you receive His promises.

Bible Notebook

Use the passage you read to complete this thought and draw a picture to represent it.

Being in God's family means that I receive _____.
(Belonging, forgiveness, the Holy Spirit, wisdom, etc.)

DAY 3

Declare   Say "I am adopted into God's family" three times.

Sing   Sing the song "Good Good Father" and follow along with the lyrics sheet.

Read   Read John 14:15-18.

           When Jesus left the earth, He told His disciples that He wasn't leaving them as orphans. The Holy Spirit came to be their Helper and Comforter.

Discuss   Have you ever felt lonely? Who or what helped you with your feelings?

           What can you do to help you remember that the Holy Spirit is always with you?

Beauty   Observe *Christ and the Children of All Races* by Vittorio Bianchini.
           Does this picture remind you of anything you have seen or read before?

Recite   Recite Romans 8:15.

Pray   Thank God for adopting you and sending the Holy Spirit to be with you always.

           Ask God to help you remember He is with you when you are afraid or lonely.

Dig Deeper

Do a poet study about the inspiring life of Fanny Crosby by searching online for her biography and more of her poems. Look specifically for the poem she wrote at age eight that begins, "Oh, what a happy soul I am."

Identity: I am adopted into God's family.

DAY 4

Declare — Say "I am adopted into God's family" three times.

Sing — Sing the song "Good Good Father" and follow along with the lyrics sheet.

Read — Read Mark 3:31-35.

Jesus makes the point that when we are followers of God, we have a spiritual family—all believers! We gain a heavenly Father and brothers and sisters in Christ all over the world when we choose to become Christians.

Discuss — Talk about the diversity in your friend groups or church family (nationalities, ages, interests).

How can we show our brothers and sisters in Christ we love and value them like family?

Beauty — Read "Redeemed, How I Love to Proclaim It" by Fanny Cosby.
Recite any portions from memory or copy your favorite stanza.

Recite — Recite Romans 8:15.

Pray — Thank God for some specific families or friends who are your brothers and sisters in Christ.

Pray for the church around the world, and specifically any countries or people groups you have a relationship with or connection to.

Family Connection

Brainstorm how you can bless another family in the body of Christ with an encouraging letter, homemade baked goods, or an act of service, and make a plan to do it.

DAY 5

Declare — Say "I am adopted into God's family" three times.

Sing — Sing the song "Good Good Father" and follow along with the lyrics sheet.

Read — Read 1 Corinthians 12:12-27.

As Christians, we are all one in Christ. We all have different roles to play, but all are important. It is important that we value all members of the body of Christ and work together.

Discuss — Talk about what gifts each member of your family has to contribute to the body of Christ (encouragement, hospitality, etc.)

What goal is the body of Christ is trying to accomplish together?

Beauty — Replicate a portion or all of this week's artwork or draw or paint what you imagine when you read this week's poem.

Recite — Recite Romans 8:15.

Pray — Thank God for the body of Christ.

Ask God to help you know how to use your gifts to strengthen and encourage God's family and reach the lost.

Demonstrate

Do a puzzle together but secretly remove a few pieces before starting. As you are finishing the puzzle, talk about how all of the pieces are needed to complete the picture. Then return the pieces and connect this to how all believers are essential in God's family.

Identity:
I am God's friend.

Declaration: I am God's friend.

Song: "What a Friend"

Verse: John 15:15

Poem: "A Friend of Jesus, O What Bliss" by Joseph C. Ludgate

Artwork: *Jesus Washing Peter's Feet* by Ford Madox Brown

No longer do I call you servants, for the servant does not know what his master is doing; but I have called you friends, for all that I have heard from my Father I have made known to you.

John 15:15

What a Friend

What a friend we have in Jesus
What a friend we have in Jesus
What a friend we have in Jesus
What a friend
(repeat)

Greater love has no man
Than he who lays down his life for a friend
(repeat)

What a friend we have in Jesus
What a friend we have in Jesus
What a friend we have in Jesus
What a friend

Greater love has no man
Than he who lays down his life for a friend
(repeat)

And I sing hallelujah, hallelujah
Hallelujah, hallelujah
(repeat)

A friend of Jesus! O what bliss
That one, so vile as I,
Should ever have a friend like this
To lead me to the sky!

Friendship with Jesus, fellowship divine,
O what blessed, sweet communion,
Jesus is a friend of mine!

A friend when other friendships cease,
A friend when others fail,
A friend who gives me joy and peace,
A friend who will prevail.

A friend when sickness lays me low,
A friend when death draws near,
A friend as through the vale I go,
A friend to help and cheer.

A friend when life's short race is o'er,
A friend when earth is past,
A friend to meet on Heaven's shore,
A friend when home at last.

"A Friend of Jesus! O What Bliss"
by Joseph C. Ludgate

Identity: I am God's friend.

Jesus Washing Peter's Feet by Ford Madox Brown
ca. 1852-1886

DAY 1

Declare   Say "I am God's friend" three times.

Sing   Sing the song "What a Friend" and follow along with the lyrics sheet.

Read   Read Genesis 22:1-19 and James 2:21-23.

Abraham obeyed and trusted God, even in a really tough situation. Because of this, God called him "friend." Obeying and trusting God unlocks the door to being close friends with God. God wants to be more than our master—He wants to be our friend.

Discuss   Who is your best friend? What makes them such a good friend?

Have you been in a situation where it was hard to trust God? What did you do?

Beauty   Observe *Jesus Washing Peter's Feet* by Ford Madox Brown.
Play Hide & Describe.

Recite   Recite John 15:15.

Pray   Ask God if there is anything He is asking you to do that you are missing.

Tell God you want to trust and obey no matter what.

Thank God for wanting to be your friend and making a way through Jesus.

Role Play

Act out the story of Abraham and Isaac that you read today. Be creative using props like a couch for the altar and a stuffed animal for the ram. Talk about how Abraham must have felt.

DAY 2

Declare — Say "I am God's friend" three times.

Sing — Sing the song "What a Friend" and follow along with the lyrics sheet.

Read — Read John 15:1-11.

Jesus tells His disciples to abide in His love and to bear fruit. Abiding in Him means having an ongoing relationship with Him—talking to Him, reading His word, obeying His commands, and worshiping Him. This is how we grow our friendship with God. When we do that, we bear fruit in our lives.

Discuss — Talk about what it means to "bear fruit" and discuss examples of fruit like good deeds, joy, peace, etc.

How do you cultivate your friendship with God? How could you nurture it more?

Beauty — Read "A Friend of Jesus! O What Bliss" by Ford Madox Brown.
Discuss any unknown vocabulary and meanings.

Recite — Recite John 15:15.

Pray — Tell God you want to get closer to Him through worship, prayer, and reading His word.

Ask God to produce the fruits of the Spirit in you.

Create

Draw or paint a picture of a vine with leaves and fruit. Use books or the internet for inspiration. Write John 15:5 somewhere on the paper.

DAY 3

Declare   Say "I am God's friend" three times.

Sing   Sing the song "What a Friend" and follow along with the lyrics sheet.

Read   Read John 15:12-17.

Jesus shows us the ultimate example of a good friend through His relationships with the disciples and by laying down His life for us. The best way we can respond to God's friendship is to lay down our lives for Him and others.

Discuss   What does it mean to "lay down our lives" for our friends? How does this relate to our friendship with God? With others?

Is there any area in your life you should be surrendering to God that you aren't?

Beauty   Observe *Jesus Washing Peter's Feet* by Ford Madox Brown. What emotions do you think the people feel in this piece?

Recite   Recite John 15:15.

Pray   Thank Jesus for being the perfect example of a friend and for laying down His life for you.

Ask God to help you love your friends as He did.

Language Arts

Think of a friend who loves like Jesus does. Write them a letter telling them what a good friend they are and thanking them for their friendship. Send it to them in the mail.

DAY 4

Declare   Say "I am God's friend" three times.

Sing   Sing the song "What a Friend" and follow along with the lyrics sheet.

Read   Read John 13:1-15.

Jesus shocked the disciples by offering to wash their feet because it was the job of the lowliest of servants, and He was God! He did it to show them an example of love, humility, and true servanthood. It set an example of how we should serve others in our lives.

Discuss   Imagine you were there at the time of this story. How would you feel about Jesus washing your feet?

How can you metaphorically "wash someone's feet" in your home today?

Beauty   Read "A Friend of Jesus! O What Bliss" by Ford Madox Brown.
Recite any portions from memory or copy your favorite stanza.

Recite   Recite John 15:15.

Pray   Confess any areas of your life that you have been prideful or selfish.

Ask God to help you think of others above yourself and serve like He did.

Bible Notebook

Write a summary of the story you read today and draw a picture to represent it.

DAY 5

Declare — Say "I am God's friend" three times.

Sing — Sing the song "What a Friend" and follow along with the lyrics sheet.

Read — Read John 14:21-26, John 15:15, and Psalm 25:14.

When we become disciples of Jesus, the Holy Spirit comes to us and lives in us to teach us, comfort us, and guide us. Being God's friend means we get to know His heart, ways, and secrets.

Discuss — Has anyone ever told you a secret? How did you feel knowing they chose to tell you?

What is the difference between a servant and a friend?

What kind of secrets do you think God would want to tell his people?

Beauty — Replicate a portion or all of this week's artwork or draw or paint what you imagine when you read this week's poem.

Recite — Recite John 15:15.

Pray — Thank God for the gift of the Holy Spirit and for all He does for you.

Tell God you want to know more of His heart and ways.

Dig Deeper

Look up Galatians 5:16-25 and talk about the fruits of the Spirit that are produced in us as we abide in Him.

Identity:
I was made to worship.

Declaration: I was made to worship.

Song: "Give Us Clean Hands"

Verse: Colossians 1:16

Poem: "Beautiful Savior" by Joseph Augustus Seiss

Artwork: *David Playing the Harp* by Jan de Bray

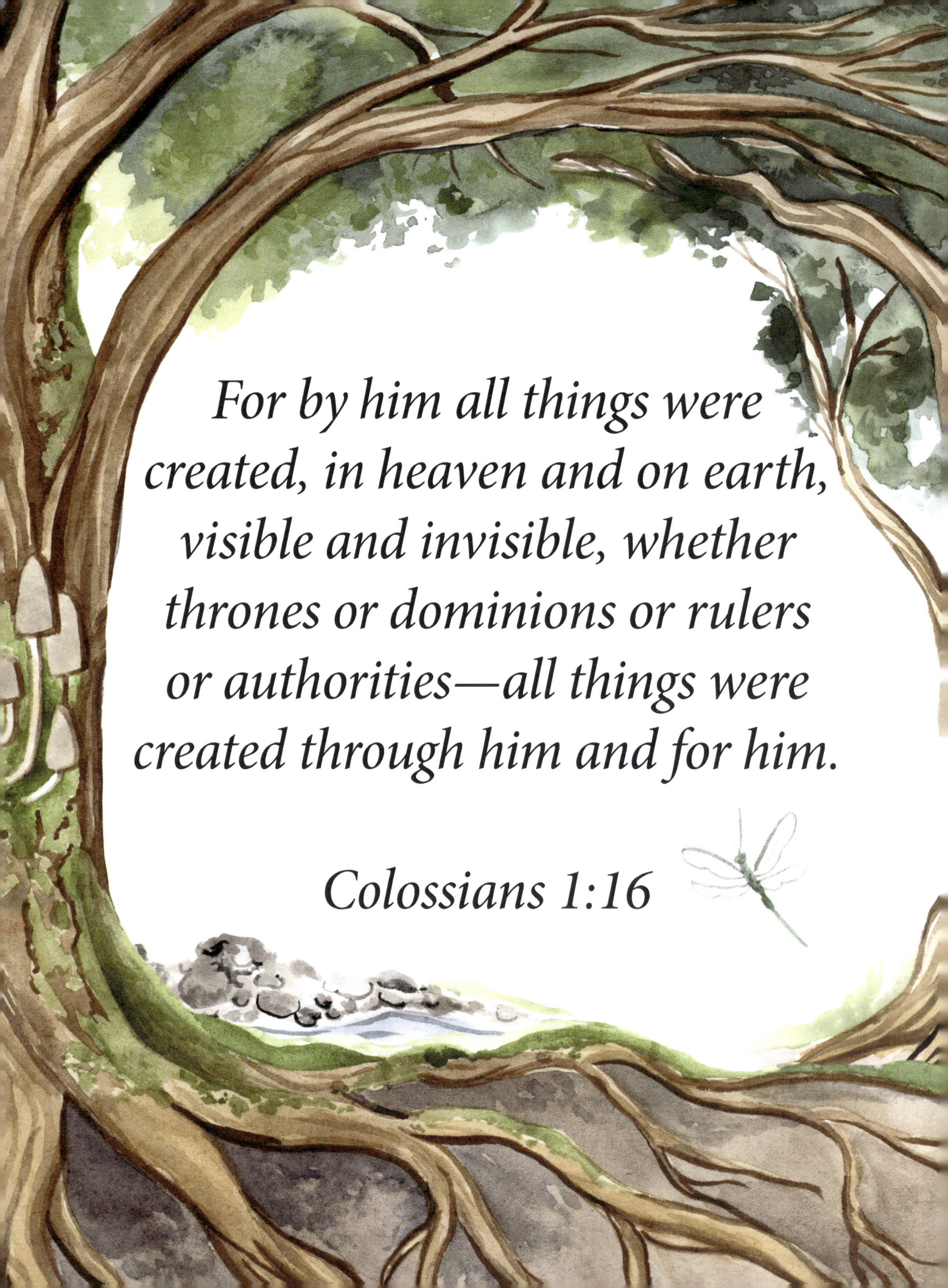

For by him all things were created, in heaven and on earth, visible and invisible, whether thrones or dominions or rulers or authorities—all things were created through him and for him.

Colossians 1:16

Give Us Clean Hands

We bow our hearts, we bend our knees
Oh Spirit come make us humble
We turn our eyes from evil things
Oh Lord we cast down our idols

Give us clean hands
Give us pure hearts
Let us not lift our souls to another
(repeat)

We bow our hearts, we bend our knees
Oh Spirit come make us humble
We turn our eyes from evil things
Oh Lord we cast down our idols

Give us clean hands
Give us pure hearts
Let us not lift our souls to another
(repeat)

And God let us be
A generation that seeks
That seeks Your face
Oh, God of Jacob
(repeat)

Beautiful Savior, King of creation,
Son of God and Son of Man!
Truly I'd love Thee, truly I'd serve thee,
Light of my soul, my Joy, my Crown.

Fair are the meadows, Fair are the woodlands,
Robed in flow'rs of blooming spring;
Jesus is fairer, Jesus is purer;
He makes our sorr'wing spirit sing.

Fair is the sunshine, Fair is the moonlight,
Bright the sparkling stars on high;
Jesus shines brighter, Jesus shines purer
Than all the angels in the sky.

Beautiful Savior, Lord of the nations,
Son of God and Son of Man!
Glory and honor, Praise, adoration,
Now and forevermore be Thine!

"Beautiful Savior"
by Joseph Augustus Seiss

David Playing the Harp by Jan de Bray
ca. 1670

DAY 1

Declare Say "I was made to worship" three times.

Sing Sing the song "Give Us Clean Hands" and follow along with the lyrics sheet.

Read Read Psalm 115 and Psalm 24:3-6.

God made all humans to worship Him. Every person worships something, even if they don't realize it. To worship something means to make it the most important thing in your life—to trust, rely on, and revere something. When we make God the most important thing in our hearts, we are doing what we were made to do.

Discuss Talk about the physical idols the Israelites worshiped in the Old Testament and the satirical message of the foolishness of idol worship in verses Psalm 115:4-8.

What are some modern-day idols that people worship in our culture?

Beauty Observe *David Playing the Harp* by Jan de Bray.
Play Hide & Describe.

Recite Recite Colossians 1:16.

Pray Praise God for being the Creator of everything and for having a purpose for man—to worship and glorify Him.

Tell God you want to use your life to worship Him and nothing/no one else.

Dig Deeper

Read Psalm 100 and Psalm 145 and talk about the different ways and reasons for worshipping the Lord.

DAY 2

Declare — Say "I was made to worship" three times.

Sing — Sing the song "Give Us Clean Hands" and follow along with the lyrics sheet.

Read — Read Colossians 3:12-17 and 1 Corinthians 10:31.

There are many ways we can worship God. Many people think of singing and playing instruments as worshiping God, but that is only one way. Worship is any time we are honoring God and bringing Him glory. For example, you worship God when you save money to give to the poor or when you put your sibling above yourself.

Discuss — What does it mean to glorify God "in word and deed" in verse 17?

Talk about various ways to worship God. Tell a story about how you worshiped God in a unique way.

Beauty — Read "Beautiful Savior" by Joseph Augustus Seiss.
Discuss any unknown vocabulary and meanings.

Recite — Recite Colossians 1:16.

Pray — Worship God by telling Him how wonderful He is and why you are thankful for Him.

Ask God to help you bring Him glory in every area of your life.

Bible Notebook

Think about how you can glorify God with your home, toys, money, time, and talents. Write about some of them by completing this sentence: "I can worship God by _____." Illustrate what you wrote.

DAY 3

Declare — Say "I was made to worship" three times.

Sing — Sing the song "Give Us Clean Hands" and follow along with the lyrics sheet.

Read — Read Psalm 19:1-6.

One way we can worship God is by acknowledging His wonder and beauty through studying and enjoying nature. When something like a sunset or the details of a flower amaze us, we can pause and praise the Creator as an act of worship.

Discuss — Talk about a time you were in awe of something that God made.

What elements in nature show God's power? Beauty? Creativity?

Beauty — Observe *David Playing the Harp* by Jan de Bray. What instruments do you see? What do you think David is thinking about?

Recite — Recite Colossians 1:16.

Pray — Praise God specifically for what you love in nature. Tell Him how incredible He is!

Ask God to reveal himself through nature to people around the world who don't know Him.

Nature Study

Go outside in your backyard or on a nature walk. Find something that amazes you that God made (an insect, flower, etc.). Try to identify what it is and learn more about it on the internet or in books.

DAY 4

Declare   Say "I was made to worship" three times.

Sing   Sing the song "Give Us Clean Hands" and follow along with the lyrics sheet.

Read   Read Mark 12:41-44.

One way we worship is by giving. We can give our money, possessions, time, devotion, and talents to glorify God. In this story, the widow didn't have much, but she gave all that she had, which meant so much to Jesus. It's not about how much we have to give, but that we give all that we have to be used by Him.

Discuss   How can you give what you have for God's glory?

Brainstorm ways you and your family can give money to the needy or spread the gospel in your city or the world.

Beauty   Read "Beautiful Savior" by Joseph Augustus Seiss.
Recite any portions from memory or copy your favorite stanza.

Recite   Recite Colossians 1:16.

Pray   Tell God you want to give Him all of you—your heart and all you have.

Ask God to show you if there is something He is asking you to give to someone else.

Bible Notebook

Write a summary of the story you read today and draw a picture to represent it.

DAY 5

Declare Say "I was made to worship" three times.

Sing Sing the song "Give Us Clean Hands" and follow along with the lyrics sheet.

Read Read Psalm 63, Acts 13:22, and John 4:23-24.

David was a man who loved God and offered up his life as worship. He expressed this worship through repentance, obedience, faith, and devotion to God. He shared his heart with God through writing, playing, and singing songs. David wrote most of the book of Psalms.

Discuss Brainstorm how each member of your family can worship God in a way that expresses themselves and their natural inclinations (through art, music, nature, giving, etc.).

What does it mean to worship in spirit and in truth? How did David exemplify that?

Beauty Replicate a portion or all of this week's artwork or draw or paint what you imagine when you read this week's poem.

Recite Recite John 15:15.

Pray Tell God you want to be a person after His heart, like David.

Worship God in spirit and in truth as you praise Him for who He is and what He has done in your family or life.

Language Arts

Write your own psalm of praise to God. Read it aloud as a poem or put a tune to it and sing it! Use the Psalms to give you ideas to get started.

Devotion:
I will love the Lord with all my heart, soul, mind and strength.

Declaration: I love the Lord with all my heart, soul, mind and strength.

Hymn: "I Love You Lord"

Verse: Luke 10:27

Poem: "My Jesus, I Love Thee" by William R. Featherston

Artwork: *Mary Magdalen Washing Christ's Feet* by Victor Wolfvoet

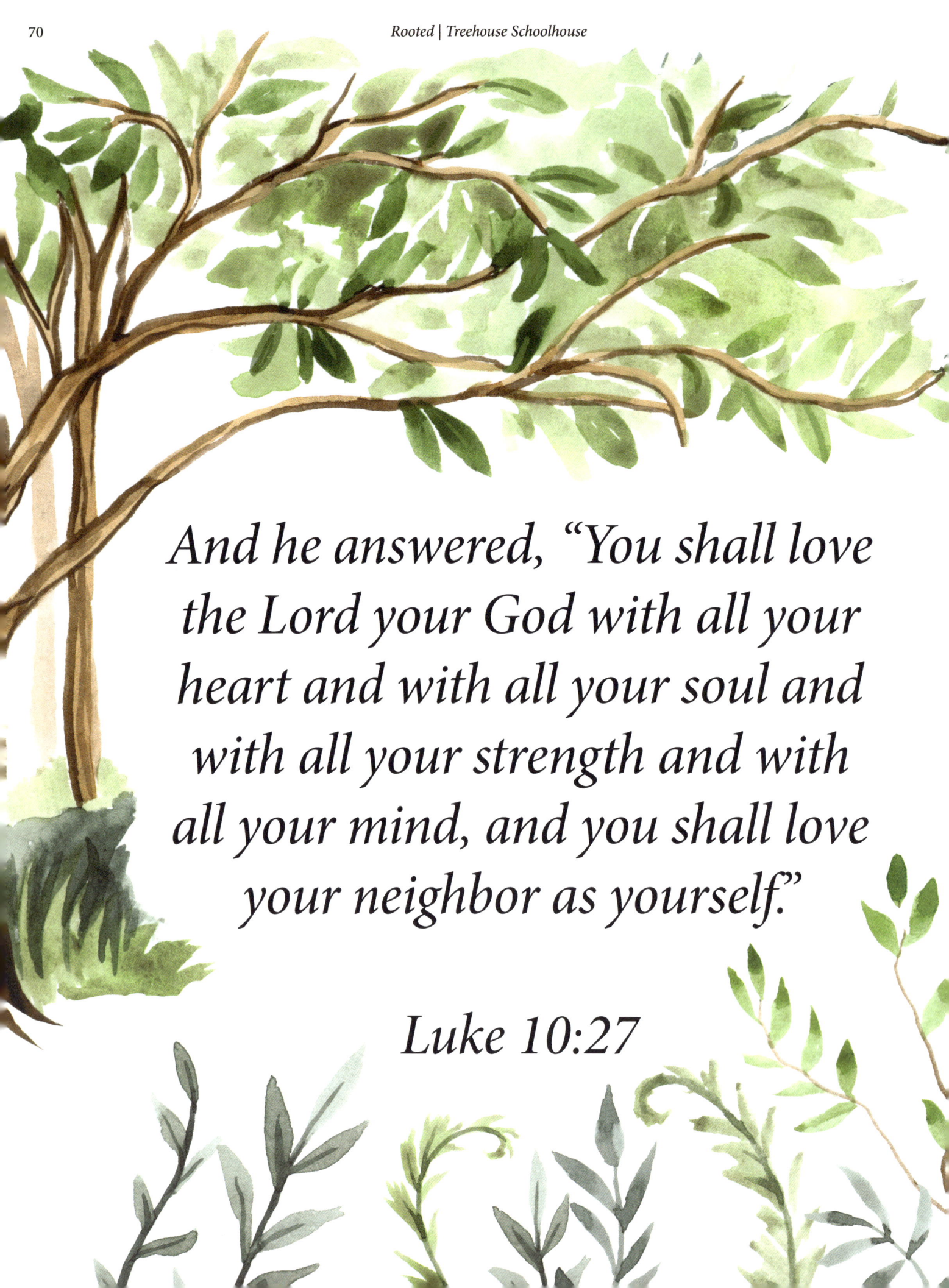

And he answered, "You shall love the Lord your God with all your heart and with all your soul and with all your strength and with all your mind, and you shall love your neighbor as yourself."

Luke 10:27

Devotion: I will love the Lord with all my heart, soul, mind, and strength.

I Love You Lord

I love You, Lord
And I lift my voice
To worship You
Oh, my soul rejoice

Take joy, my King
In what You hear
May it be a sweet
Sweet sound in Your ear

I love You, Lord
And I lift my voice
To worship You
Oh, my soul rejoice

Take joy, my King
In what You hear
May it be a sweet
Sweet sound in Your ear

May it be a sweet, sweet sound
May it be a sweet, sweet sound
May it be a sweet, sweet sound in Your ear

My Jesus, I love Thee, I know Thou art mine;
For Thee all the follies of sin I resign;
My gracious Redeemer, my Savior art Thou;
If ever I loved Thee, my Jesus, 'tis now.

I love Thee because Thou hast first loved me,
And purchased my pardon on Calvary's tree;
I love Thee for wearing the thorns on Thy brow;
If ever I loved Thee, my Jesus, 'tis now.

I'll love Thee in life, I will love Thee in death,
And praise Thee as long as Thou lendest me breath;
And say when the death dew lies cold on my brow,
If ever I loved Thee, my Jesus, 'tis now.

In mansions of glory and endless delight,
I'll ever adore Thee in heaven so bright;
I'll sing with the glittering crown on my brow,
If ever I loved Thee, my Jesus, 'tis now.

"My Jesus, I Love Thee"
by William R. Featherston

Devotion: I will love the Lord with all my heart, soul, mind, and strength.

Mary Magdalen Washing Christ's Feet by Victor Wolfvoet ca. 1639 and 1662

DAY 1

Declare Say "I will love the Lord with all my heart, soul, mind, and strength" three times.

Sing Sing the hymn "I Love You Lord" and follow along with the lyrics sheet.

Read Read Luke 10:25-28.

The most important thing we can do with our lives is to love God with all of who we are—all of our heart, our soul, our mind, and our strength. This is the foundation to receiving eternal life and living a full life with God on earth.

Discuss What does it mean to love God in each of these areas?

Can you think of someone in your life that you believe loves God with all of themselves? Who is it and what makes their life stand out to you?

Beauty Observe *Mary Magdalen Washing Christ's Feet* by Victor Wolfvoet.
Play Hide & Describe.

Recite Recite Luke 10:27.

Pray Tell God how much you love Him. Name some reasons why you love Him.

Ask God to help you love Him with all of yourself.

Bible Notebook

Write Luke 10:27 in your Bible Notebook. Draw a picture of yourself and label different areas of your body with the words mind, heart, soul, strength.

Devotion: I will love the Lord with all my heart, soul, mind, and strength.

DAY 2

Declare — Say "I will love the Lord with all my heart, soul, mind, and strength" three times.

Sing — Sing the hymn "I Love You Lord" and follow along with the lyrics sheet.

Read — Read Psalm 28:7 and Proverbs 4:23.

When God talks about your heart, He does not mean the organ inside of your chest that pumps blood. Loving God with all of your heart and soul means to love Him with sincerity, devotion, and with all of your emotions.

Discuss — Talk about a time you had a big emotion and you paused to pray about it or allowed it to point you to God.

Discuss what the various emotions are and what it would look like to acknowledge God in each of them.

Beauty — Read "My Jesus, I Love Thee" by William R. Featherston.
Discuss any unknown vocabulary and meanings.

Recite — Recite Luke 10:27.

Pray — Tell God He is worthy of being involved in all the areas of your emotions and heart.

Thank God for being trustworthy and safe with your heart and soul when you pour it out to Him.

Play

Play a game of "Emotions Charades." Write down various emotions and take turns drawing and acting them out. Discuss how you could turn each emotion into worship and trust in God as you play.

DAY 3

Declare   Say "I will love the Lord with all my heart, soul, mind, and strength" three times.

Sing   Sing the hymn "I Love You Lord" and follow along with the lyrics sheet.

Read   Read Proverbs 3:5-6, Isaiah 55:8-9, and Philippians 4:8.

We show God's love when we trust His thoughts and ways over our own. We love God with our mind when we think highly of Him and continually fill our minds with truth.

Discuss   Share about a time you fought against a lie with truth.

Can you think of a Bible story when God's ways were higher than man's?

Beauty   Observe *Mary Magdalen Washing Christ's Feet* by Victor Wolfvoet. If you could walk into this picture, how would you feel and what would you do?

Recite   Recite Luke 10:27.

Pray   Ask God for help to combat lies. Name them specifically and ask for truth to replace them.

Tell God you desire to love Him with your whole mind by thinking on truth and trusting Him and not your own thoughts.

Dig Deeper

Practice loving God with your mind by doing some digging in the Word. What is something you want to know about God or his ways? Go on a quest in the Bible to find answers.

DAY 4

Declare Say "I will love the Lord with all my heart, soul, mind, and strength" three times.

Sing Sing the hymn "I Love You Lord" and follow along with the lyrics sheet.

Read Psalm 62:5-8 and James 1:2-4.

Loving God with our strength means giving Him our energy, talents, physical strength, and abilities. It also means standing strong in loving Him, even when it's difficult.

Discuss Have you ever had a hard time trusting or loving God but stood strong in doing it anyway?

What talent or ability do you have that you could use to worship and love God with? How can you do that this week?

Beauty Read "My Jesus, I love Thee" by William R. Featherston.
Recite any portions from memory or copy your favorite stanza.

Recite Recite Luke 10:27.

Pray Ask God to help you love Him with all of your strength—your talents, abilities, and body.

Ask God to improve the ways you show Him love with how you live your life.

Family Connection

Brainstorm together some ways you can love God together as a family this week and make a plan to do it. Some ideas: serving another family, having a worship night, or sharing the gospel with a neighbor.

DAY 5

Declare   Say "I will love the Lord with all my heart, soul, mind, and strength" three times.

Sing   Sing the hymn "I Love You Lord" and follow along with the lyrics sheet.

Read   Read John 12:1-7.

Mary didn't care who was around or what anyone would think. She poured out costly perfume on Jesus' feet and wiped it with her hair. The perfume was worth around a year of wages. She deeply loved Jesus and was willing to give everything she had to show it. Sometimes showing our love to God will cost us something.

Discuss   How does this story remind you of what we have been learning all week?

Why do you think it's significant how much the perfume costs?

When does it "cost something" to show our love to God?

Beauty   Replicate a portion or all of this week's artwork or draw or paint what you imagine when you read this week's poem.

Recite   Recite Luke 10:27.

Pray   Ask God to help you give everything you have to show Him your love, no matter the cost.

Thank God for all that He is and express your love to Him in your own words.

Bible Notebook

Write a summary of the story you read today and draw a picture to represent it.

Devotion:
I will seek first the kingdom of God in all I do.

Declaration: I will seek first the kingdom of God in all I do.

Song: "Do Not Worry"

Verse: Matthew 6:33

Poem: "His Eye is on the Sparrow" by C. D. Martin

Artwork: *Christ and the Rich Young Ruler* by Heinrich Hofmann

But seek first the kingdom of God and His righteousness, and all these things will be added to you.

Matthew 6:33

Do Not Worry

See the birds that are singing in the spring air?
They're given everything they need
They don't worry where their next meal will come from
They don't worry 'bout a thing

So just look around you and try to listen to
The song creation sings
And don't you worry 'cause you're in the hands
Of the God who made everything

See the flowers in their colorful beauty
They're dressed better than a king
They don't worry about what they should wear, no
They don't worry 'bout a thing

So just look around you and try to listen to
The song creation sings
And don't you worry 'cause you're in the hands
Of the God who made everything

Because you're not a bird and you're not a flower
You don't have petals or wings
But there is good news, you're worth so much more
To the God who made everything

So when you worry 'bout today or tomorrow
And the storms that they might bring
Try to remember that you're in the hands
Of the God who made every single thing

Why should I feel discouraged,
Why should the shadows come,
Why should my heart be lonely
And long for Heav'n and home,
When Jesus is my portion?
My constant Friend is He:
His eye is on the sparrow,
And I know He watches me;
His eye is on the sparrow,
And I know He watches me.

"Let not your heart be troubled,"
His tender word I hear,
And resting on His goodness,
I lose my doubts and fears:
Tho' by the path He leadeth
But one step I may see:
His eye is on the sparrow,
And I know He watches me;
His eye is on the sparrow,
And I know He watches me.

Whenever I am tempted,
Whenever clouds arise,
When songs give place to sighing,
When hope within me dies,
I draw the closer to Him,
From care He sets me free;
His eye is on the sparrow,
And I know He cares for me;
His eye is on the sparrow,
And I know He cares for me.

"His Eye is on the Sparrow"
by C. D. Martin

Devotion: I will seek first the kingdom of God in all I do.

Christ and the Rich Young Ruler by Heinrich Hofmann ca. 1881

DAY 1

Declare — Say "I will seek first the kingdom of God in all I do" three times.

Sing — Sing the song "Do Not Worry" and follow along with the lyrics sheet.

Read — Read 1 Chronicles 29:10-13 and Psalm 95:1-7.

The kingdom of God refers to God's reign—in heaven and on earth. We acknowledge and worship Him as King of the heavens, the earth, and of our own lives when we choose to seek Him and His plans for our lives above our own.

Discuss — Talk about kings. Can you think of a king you have read about in a story? Compare his leadership to God's as King.

How does it make you feel to know God is ruler of all?

Beauty — Observe *Christ and the Rich Young Ruler* by Heinrich Hofmann.
Play Hide & Describe.

Recite — Recite Matthew 6:33.

Pray — Praise God for being such a strong and mighty king!

Tell God you want Him to be king of your heart and life.

Create

Paint or draw a nature scene, including mountains and/or water. Copy Psalm 95:4-5 somewhere on the paper.

DAY 2

Declare Say "I will seek first the kingdom of God in all I do" three times.

Sing Sing the song "Do Not Worry" and follow along with the lyrics sheet.

Read Read Matthew 6:25-34.

Jesus tells us to let go of worry and anxiety and put all of our trust in Him as King and provider. Jesus compares us to the birds of the air and the flowers of the field, who do absolutely nothing to be taken care of. The challenge for us is to shift our focus from seeking our own kingdom to seeking first *His* kingdom.

Discuss Talk about a time when God provided for you.

What are some things you find yourself worrying about?

Discuss what it means to "seek first the kingdom of God" versus our "own kingdom."

Beauty Read "His Eye is on the Sparrow" by C. D. Martin.
Discuss any unknown vocabulary and meanings.

Recite Recite Matthew 6:33.

Pray Ask God to help you lay down your worries and fears and trust Him more.

Praise God for being such a wonderful provider.

Dig Deeper

Read Matthew 6:29-31. Do some research on the internet about the history and inspiration of the poem/hymn "His Eye is on the Sparrow."

DAY 3

Declare   Say "I will seek first the kingdom of God in all I do" three times.

Sing   Sing the song "Do Not Worry" and follow along with the lyrics sheet.

Read   Read Matthew 19:16-24.

       Money is not inherently good or bad, but if it is more important to us than God, it is an idol. In this parable the man chooses his possessions and money over following Jesus.

Discuss   Talk about idols. What are the common seen and unseen idols people worship in our culture?

       How can we use money to serve the purposes of God and advance the kingdom, rather than become a hindrance?

Beauty   Observe *Christ and the Rich Young Ruler* by Heinrich Hofmann. What emotions do you see in this picture?

Recite   Recite Matthew 6:33.

Pray   Ask God to help you love and value Him more than any earthly possession.

       Ask God to help you be a good steward of your money and use it for His purposes.

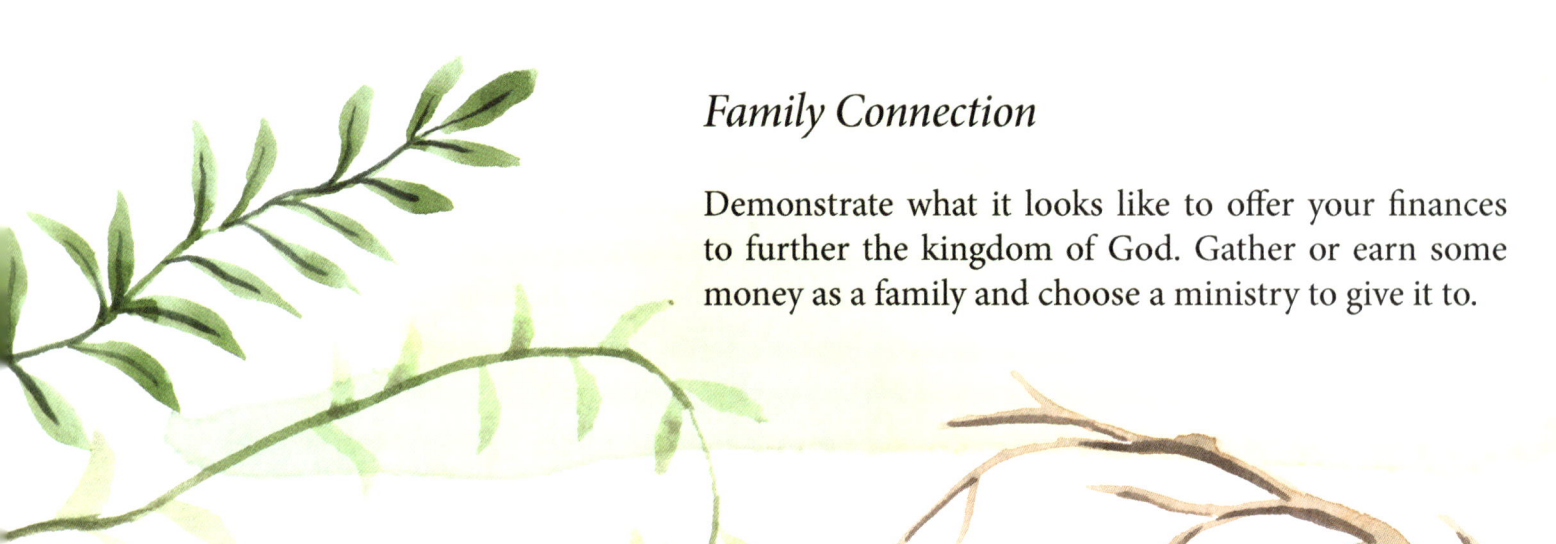

Family Connection

Demonstrate what it looks like to offer your finances to further the kingdom of God. Gather or earn some money as a family and choose a ministry to give it to.

DAY 4

Declare — Say "I will seek first the kingdom of God in all I do" three times.

Sing — Sing the song "Do Not Worry" and follow along with the lyrics sheet.

Read — Read Psalm 27:7-8, James 4:8, and Jeremiah 29:13.

The Bible tells us that when we seek God, He will respond. We seek God when we get to know Him and His ways. We seek God by praying, worshipping, reading the Bible, and following His guidance for our lives. When we pursue Him, we will find Him.

Discuss — Talk about a time you sought after God. What does it look like to "find God"?

In what ways can you actively seek God in your life?

Beauty — Read "His Eye is on the Sparrow" by C. D. Martin.
Recite any portions from memory or copy your favorite stanza.

Recite — Recite Matthew 6:33.

Pray — Thank God for being a God who responds when we seek Him.

Tell God you love Him and want to know Him more.

Play

Write Matthew 6:33 on a piece of paper and cut out each word. Hide each word separately as "treasures" for your children to seek. Once found, have them unscramble the passage in order.

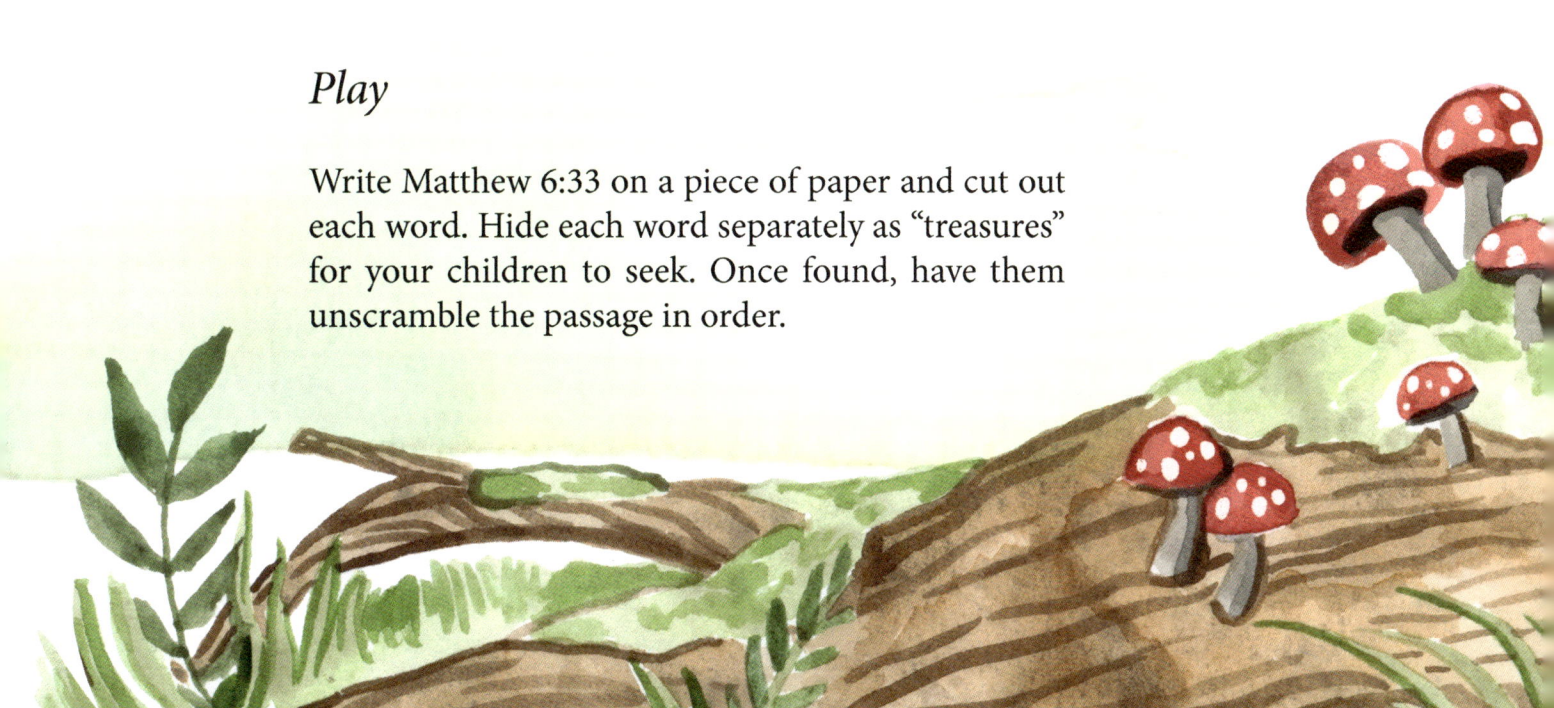

DAY 5

Declare — Say "I will seek first the kingdom of God in all I do" three times.

Sing — Sing the song "Do Not Worry" and follow along with the lyrics sheet.

Read — Read Matthew 13:44-46.

These two short parables talk about the value and the cost of the kingdom of God. In both parables the man seeks the treasure and in both, the man sells all he has to buy it. Jesus tells these stories to teach us that following Him will cost us everything, but is worth it all.

Discuss — Talk about a time you lost something. To what lengths did you go to in order to find it?

What does it look like to seek or search for God's kingdom?

What does following Jesus "cost"?

Beauty — Replicate a portion or all of this week's artwork or draw or paint what you imagine when you read this week's poem.

Recite — Recite Matthew 6:33.

Pray — Tell Jesus He is the treasure and is worth everything you have to give.

Ask Jesus to help you always seek Him first, no matter the cost.

Bible Notebook

Write a summary of the story you read today and draw a picture to represent it.

Devotion:
I will trust God in good times and bad.

Declaration: I will trust God in good times and bad.

Song: "Tis So Sweet"

Verse: Isaiah 41:10

Poem: "God is Ever Good" by Anonymous

Artwork: *Joseph Recognized by his Brothers* by Charles Antoine Coypel

Fear not, for I am with you; be not dismayed, for I am your God; I will strengthen you, I will help you, I will uphold you with my righteous right hand.

Isaiah 41:10

'Tis So Sweet

'Tis so sweet to trust in Jesus
And to take Him at His Word
Just to rest upon His promise
And to know, "Thus saith the Lord"
(the Lord, the Lord)

Jesus, Jesus, how I trust Him
How I've proved Him o'er and o'er
Jesus, Jesus, precious Jesus
Oh, for grace to trust Him more
(and more and more)

Oh, how sweet to trust in Jesus
Just to trust His cleansing blood
And in simple faith to plunge me
'Neath the healing, cleansing flood
(oh, oh)

Jesus, Jesus, how I trust Him
How I've proved Him o'er and o'er
Jesus, Jesus, precious Jesus
Oh, for grace to trust Him more
(and more and more)

I'm so glad I learned to trust Thee
Precious Jesus, Savior, Friend
And I know that Thou art with me
Will be with me to the end
('til the end)

Jesus, Jesus, how I trust Him
How I've proved Him o'er and o'er
Jesus, Jesus, precious Jesus
Oh for grace to trust Him more
(repeat)

Jesus, Jesus, how I trust Him

Whene'er I tred the highway
Or pass through leafy wood,
Methinks I hear a murmur,
"God is ever good!"

He careth for the songsters
And daily gives them food;
I think I hear them singing,
"God is ever good!"

To earth He sent the Savior
(We wonder how He could)
To bear our sins and sorrows;
God is ever good.

Whene'er I count my blessings
And thank Him as I should,
My soul cries out in rapture,
"God is ever good!"

Whene'er I pass through trials,
And trust Him as I should,
My heart is filled with glory:
God is ever good.

When I have crossed the River,
And on the Shore have stood,
I still shall sing His praises—
"God is ever good!"

"God is Ever Good"
Anonymous

Devotion: I will trust God in good times and bad.

Joseph Recognized by his Brothers by Charles Antoine Coypel

ca. 1694-1752

DAY 1

Declare — Say "I will trust God in good times and bad" three times.

Sing — Sing the hymn "Tis So Sweet" and follow along with the lyrics sheet.

Read — Read Genesis 37:5-36 and Genesis 39:1-6.

Joseph's brothers sold Joseph into slavery and then staged his death so his father wouldn't go looking for him. He could have given up all hope, but instead, he trusted God. He became the overseer of Potiphar's estate.

Discuss — Why did Joseph's brothers treat him this way? What was at the root of their actions?

Why did Potiphar trust Joseph as the overseer of the estate?

Have you ever been tempted to give up hope and stop trusting God? What did you do?

Beauty — Observe *Joseph Recognized by his Brothers* by Charles Antoine Coypel. Play Hide & Describe.

Recite — Recite Isaiah 41:10.

Pray — Ask God to help you stay steadfast in your trust in Him.

Thank God for being with you no matter what you go through in life.

Role Play

Act out the Bible story you read today. Use blankets or jackets for the coats. Make a "pit" with cushions. Appoint someone to represent Joseph, the brothers, the slave traders, and Jacob. Read or tell the story and act out the scene.

DAY 2

Declare Say "I will trust God in good times and bad" three times.

Sing Sing the hymn "Tis So Sweet" and follow along with the lyrics sheet.

Read Read Genesis 39:7-41:57.

Joseph was accused of doing something he didn't do and ended up in prison. Difficult circumstances kept happening to Joseph, but he continued to trust God. With God's wisdom, he interpreted the dreams of the prisoners and Pharaoh, which landed him a position as governor of Egypt.

Discuss Talk about a time you were accused of doing something you didn't do. How did you feel?

What do you think would have happened to Joseph if he had given up hope and stopped trusting God?

Beauty Read "God is Ever Good."
Discuss any unknown vocabulary and meanings.

Recite Recite Isaiah 41:10.

Pray Tell God about a difficult circumstance you are facing and thank Him for being with you in it.

Ask God to give you courage and strength throughout your walk with Him.

Bible Notebook / Geography

Locate Hebron, Israel on a world map or globe. Locate the Mediterranean Sea and Egypt. Joseph was sold by his brothers at Hebron and traveled by sea to Egypt.

DAY 3

Declare   Say "I will trust God in good times and bad" three times.

Sing   Sing the hymn "Tis So Sweet" and follow along with the lyrics sheet.

Read   Read Genesis 42-46 (or summarize).

Joseph's steadfastness in trusting God in hard times was the door to rescuing his family in a famine. God turned terrible circumstances in Joseph's life into something good.

Discuss   Review the full story of Joseph, pointing out how he continually trusted God in good and bad times and what came from that choice.

What does perseverance mean? How did Joseph practice perseverance?

Beauty   Observe *Joseph Recognized by his Brothers* by Charles Antoine Coypel. What emotions does this painting evoke in you?

Recite   Recite Isaiah 41:10.

Pray   Ask God to help you have perseverance in your walk with Him.

Tell God how much you love Him and trust Him with your whole heart.

Bible Notebook

Choose your favorite part of the story you have learned about Joseph and write the story in your own words in your Bible Notebook. Illustrate what you wrote.

DAY 4

Declare Say "I will trust God in good times and bad" three times.

Sing Sing the hymn "Tis So Sweet" and follow along with the lyrics sheet.

Read Read Proverbs 3:5-6 and Romans 8:28.

Trusting God means relying on Him in all things, with all of our hearts. It also means letting go of what we know and embracing His truth and ways, even though we don't know the end of the story. When we choose to do that, He will make our paths straight and turn our difficult circumstances into good.

Discuss What area in your life do you have the hardest time trusting God?

Talk about a difficult circumstance you have gone through and what it looked like to trust God in it. Did anything good come from it?

Beauty Read "God is Ever Good."
Recite any portions from memory or copy your favorite stanza.

Recite Recite Isaiah 41:10.

Pray Thank God for being a refuge in hard times.

Ask God to help you put all of your trust in Him.

Dig Deeper / Bible Notebook

Look up and read these verses about God being our refuge:
Psalm 46:1-3, Psalm 91:2, Isaiah 25:4.

Copy one in your Bible Notebook and draw a picture.

DAY 5

Declare	Say "I will trust God in good times and bad" three times.
Sing	Sing the hymn "Tis So Sweet" and follow along with the lyrics sheet.
Read	Read Lamentations 3:22–23 and Jeremiah 29:11.
	One of the best things to do in hard times is to remember God's faithfulness and promises. God's plans for us are good—for us to prosper and have hope and a future.
Discuss	Imagine your life as an adult. What do you hope it looks like?
	Talk about the ways God has been faithful to you.
	Discuss some promises from God that you know are true.
Beauty	Replicate a portion or all of this week's artwork or draw or paint what you imagine when you read this week's poem.
Recite	Recite Isaiah 41:10.
Pray	Thank God for his promises—name some specifically.
	Ask God to help you remember His faithfulness to you in hard times.

Create

Copy Jeremiah 29:11 in the middle of the paper. Draw pictures surrounding it that represent how God has been faithful to you and kept His promises.

Devotion:
I will read and study God's word.

Declaration: I will read and study God's word.

Song: "The Word of God (Hebrews 4:12)"

Verse: 2 Timothy 3:16-17

Poem: "Thy Word Is Like a Garden, Lord" by Edwin Hodder

Artwork: *The Parable of the Sower* by Marten van Valckenborch

All Scripture is breathed out by God and profitable for teaching, for reproof, for correction, and for training in righteousness, that the man of God may be complete, equipped for every good work.

1 Timothy 3:16-17

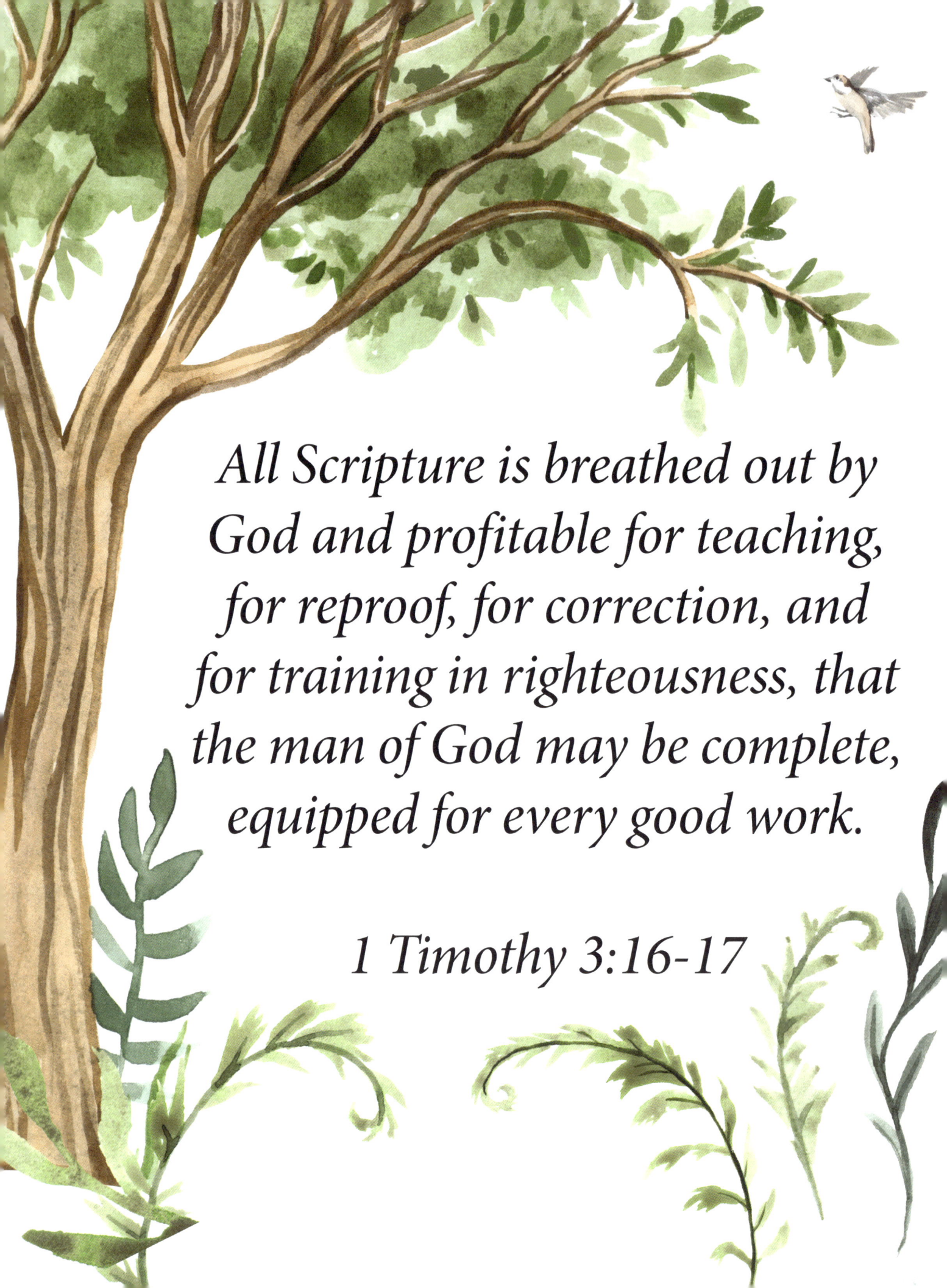

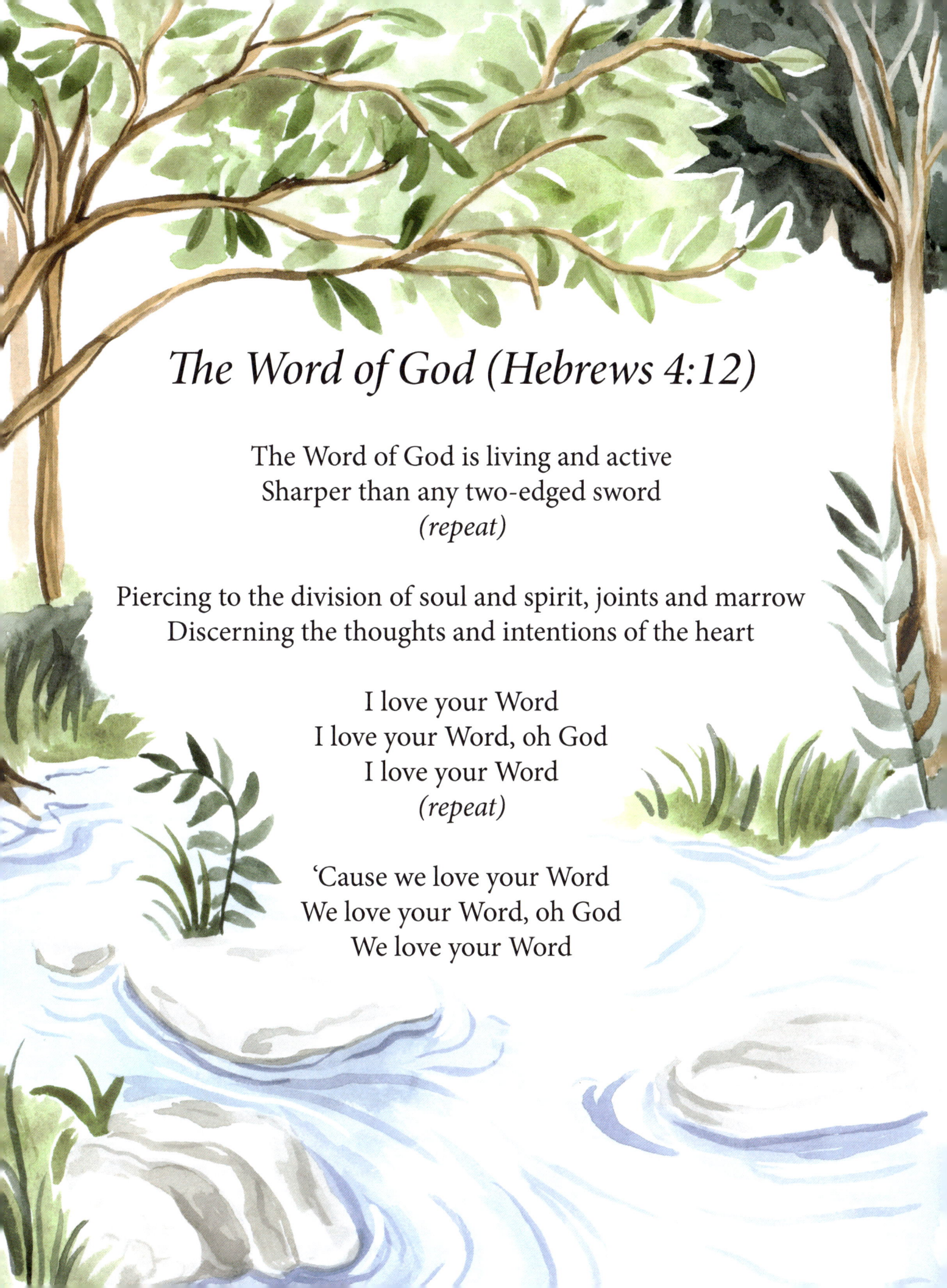

The Word of God (Hebrews 4:12)

The Word of God is living and active
Sharper than any two-edged sword
(repeat)

Piercing to the division of soul and spirit, joints and marrow
Discerning the thoughts and intentions of the heart

I love your Word
I love your Word, oh God
I love your Word
(repeat)

'Cause we love your Word
We love your Word, oh God
We love your Word

Thy Word is like a garden, Lord,
With flowers bright and fair;
And everyone who seeks may pluck
A lovely cluster there.

Thy Word is like a deep, deep mine;
And jewels rich and rare
Are hidden in its mighty depths
For every searcher there.

Thy Word is like a starry host:
A thousand rays of light
Are seen to guide the traveler
And make his pathway bright.

Thy Word is like an armory,
Where soldiers may repair
And find, for life's long battle day,
All needful weapons there.

O may I love Thy precious Word,
May I explore the mine,
May I its fragrant flowers glean,
May light upon me shine!

O may I find my armor there!
Thy Word my trusty sword,
I'll learn to fight with every foe
The battle of the Lord.

"Thy Word Is Like a Garden, Lord"
by Edwin Hodder

Devotion: I will read and study God's word.

The Parable of the Sower by Marten van Valckenborch
ca. 1580-1590

DAY 1

Declare	Say "I will read and study God's word" three times.
Sing	Sing the song "The Word of God (Hebrews 4:12)" and follow along with the lyrics sheet.
Read	Read Luke 8:1-15.
	The seed represents the Word of God, and the places the seeds fall represent our hearts. We may read, hear, and even memorize the Word of God, but the "soil" where the Word is planted is what matters.
Discuss	Relate this parable to something in your own life. (Example: A personal story or a garden experience.)
	What does the passage say happens when a seed is planted in good soil? What does that mean?
	What can you do to keep a heart that is "good soil"?
Beauty	Observe *The Parable of the Sower* by Marten van Valckenborch. Play Hide & Describe.
Recite	Recite 1 Timothy 3:16-17.
Pray	Tell God that you desire your heart to be good soil.
	Tell God that you trust Him, and ask for His help to keep the worries of the world from stealing the Word from your heart.
	Ask God to give you the courage to share the Word with others.

Bible Notebook

In your Bible Notebook, summarize the four types of soil the seeds fell on and draw a picture to represent them.

DAY 2

Declare — Say "I will read and study God's word" three times.

Sing — Sing the song "The Word of God (Hebrews 4:12)" and follow along with the lyrics sheet.

Read — Read Psalm 119:1-16.

Psalm 119 reminds us that not only are we to read God's Word, but we also should obey it. When we invest time in getting the Word of God deep into our hearts, we will be better equipped to draw on the truth throughout our lives.

Discuss — Which verses stood out to you in the reading today?

Does it sound like David dreads reading God's word or deeply desires it? What makes you think so?

How can you cultivate a hunger for God's word in your heart?

Beauty — Read "Thy Word Is Like a Garden, Lord" by Edwin Hodder. Discuss any unknown vocabulary and meanings.

Recite — Recite 1 Timothy 3:16-17.

Pray — Thank God for the gift of His Word.

Ask God to help you love His Word more.

Pray some of the verses in the passage you read today (For example, verses 10, 15-16.)

Create

Use cardstock or construction paper and other craft materials to make a bookmark for your Bible. Find Psalm 119 and bookmark it.

DAY 3

Declare Say "I will read and study God's word" three times.

Sing Sing the song "The Word of God (Hebrews 4:12)" and follow along with the lyrics sheet.

Read Read Psalm 119:97-112.

David continues to talk about his love for God's Word and all it does for him. When we live dedicated to knowing, understanding, and following God's Word, we will see the fruit in our lives. The Word of God will be like sweet honey and a light to our path.

Discuss What words does David use throughout the psalm that mean "God's Word"? (Example: precepts, statutes.)

Share stories of times you have tried to walk somewhere in the dark. What did you use to see?

How is God's Word like a lamp? How is it like honey?

Beauty Observe *The Parable of the Sower* by Marten van Valckenborch.
Why do you think the artist depicted Jesus and the crowd in the background of this piece?

Recite Recite 1 Timothy 3:16-17.

Pray Ask God to help you rely on His word in life's circumstances.

Thank God for guiding our lives by giving us His Word.

Bible Notebook

Write a new psalm to God about your love for His Word. Use Psalm 119 as inspiration. Younger students could copy verses.

Devotion: I will read and study God's word.

DAY 4

Declare Say "I will read and study God's word" three times.

Sing Sing the song "The Word of God (Hebrews 4:12)" and follow along with the lyrics sheet.

Read Read Isaiah 40:7-8, Psalm 119:89-90, and Psalm 119:160.

God's Word is the one thing we have in life we can always count on. It doesn't change or fade away. Everything on earth passes away, but God's Word is true through all generations.

Discuss Talk about a time when you experienced change and it was difficult. (Example: a move, loss of a friend, etc.)

Talk about truth. Do you think truth can evolve and change over time?

Talk about prophecies in the Old Testament and how they were fulfilled.

Beauty Read "Thy Word Is Like a Garden, Lord" by Edwin Hodder.
Recite any portions from memory or copy your favorite stanza.

Recite Recite 1 Timothy 3:16-17.

Pray Thank God for giving us His Word to rely on.

Ask God to help you remember to invest time in His Word.

Pray for the Bible to be translated into all of the languages in the world so everyone can have this gift.

Nature Study

Go outside and pick a bouquet of wildflowers or grasses. Draw a picture of something you found, identify and label it if possible. Write Isaiah 40:7-8 next to it on the page.

DAY 5

Declare — Say "I will read and study God's word" three times.

Sing — Sing the song "The Word of God (Hebrews 4:12)" and follow along with the lyrics sheet.

Read — Read Matthew 4:1-11, Hebrews 4:12, and Ephesians 6:17.

God's Word is different from any other book because it is living and accomplishes things on earth and in our lives. The Word of God is our weapon against the assaults of our spiritual enemy. Jesus used the Word of God to combat Satan when He was tempted.

Discuss — Talk about a time you heard or read a verse that "pierced" your heart.

What are some purposes of God's Word according to these verses? Can you think of more purposes it serves? (Refer to Psalm 119 and 2 Timothy 3:16-17.)

How can you combat the enemy's lies with the Word of God?

Beauty — Replicate a portion or all of this week's artwork or draw or paint what you imagine when you read this week's poem.

Recite — Recite 1 Timothy 3:16-17.

Pray — Thank God for giving us the Word as a weapon against Satan.

Ask God to give you a humble heart to receive guidance and correction from the word of God.

Play

Play "Sword Drill" by giving your children a series of verses, one by one, and having them race to find them in their Bibles. Whoever finds it first stands up and reads it. Use verses from this week's lesson or previous scripture memory passages.

Devotion:
I will talk to God and He talks to me.

Declaration: I will talk to God and He talks to me.

Song: "All the Way My Savior Leads Me"

Verse: Jeremiah 29:12-13

Poem: "I Heard the Voice of Jesus Say" by John B. Dykes

Artwork: *Samuel Relating to Eli the Judgements of God upon Eli's House* by John Singleton Copley

Then you will call upon me and come and pray to me, and I will hear you. You will seek me and find me, when you seek me with all your heart.

Jeremiah 29:12-13

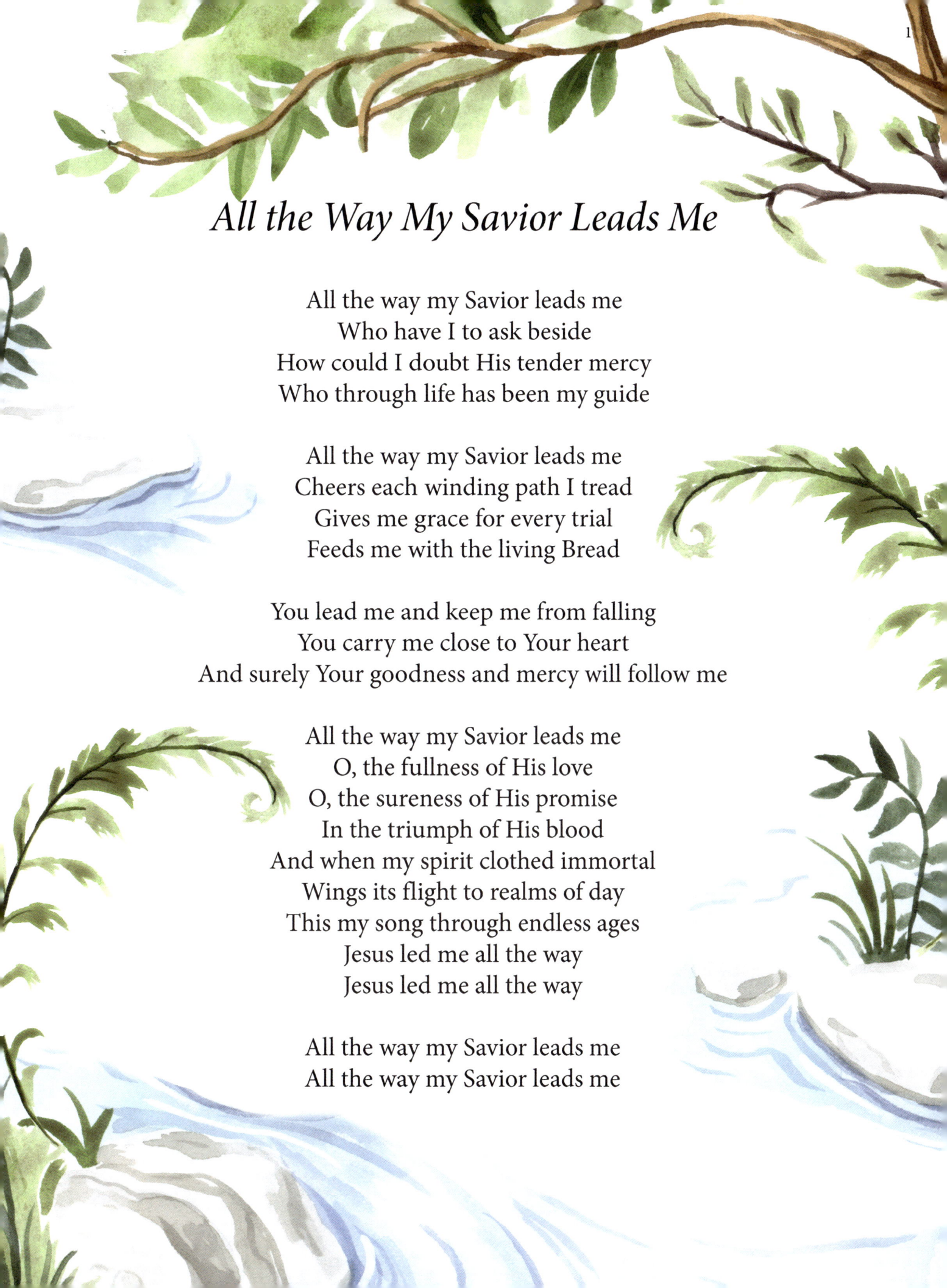

All the Way My Savior Leads Me

All the way my Savior leads me
Who have I to ask beside
How could I doubt His tender mercy
Who through life has been my guide

All the way my Savior leads me
Cheers each winding path I tread
Gives me grace for every trial
Feeds me with the living Bread

You lead me and keep me from falling
You carry me close to Your heart
And surely Your goodness and mercy will follow me

All the way my Savior leads me
O, the fullness of His love
O, the sureness of His promise
In the triumph of His blood
And when my spirit clothed immortal
Wings its flight to realms of day
This my song through endless ages
Jesus led me all the way
Jesus led me all the way

All the way my Savior leads me
All the way my Savior leads me

I heard the voice of Jesus say,
"Come unto Me and rest;
Lay down, thou weary one, lay down
Thy head upon My breast."
I came to Jesus as I was,
Weary, and worn, and sad;
I found in Him a resting place,
And He has made me glad.

I heard the voice of Jesus say,
"Behold, I freely give
The living water; thirsty one,
Stoop down and drink, and live."
I came to Jesus, and I drank
Of that life-giving stream;
My thirst was quenched, my soul revived,
And now I live in Him.

I heard the voice of Jesus say,
"I am this dark world's Light;
Look unto Me, thy morn shall rise,
And all thy day be bright."
I looked to Jesus, and I found
In Him my Star, my Sun,
And in that Light of life I'll walk,
Till traveling days are done.

"I Heard the Voice of Jesus Say"
by John B. Dykes

Devotion: I will talk to God and He talks to me. 113

Samuel Relating to Eli the Judgements of God upon Eli's House by John Singleton Copley
ca. 1780

DAY 1

Declare Say "I will talk to God and He talks to me" three times.

Sing Sing the hymn "All the Way My Savior Leads Me" and follow along with the lyrics sheet.

Read Read Philippians 4:5-7 and 1 Thessalonians 5:16-18.

These passages remind us to lay our anxieties down and instead, talk to God about them. Prayer is simply talking to God. We can come to Him in every situation and we are told to pray continually. We can pray at any time and anywhere. We can pray in our hearts, out loud, by writing, or even by singing!

Discuss Think about how you usually spend your days. Where could you routinely add in talking to God? (While you lay in bed at night, while you ride in the car, etc.)

What do you worry about that you can let go of and ask God to replace with peace?

Beauty Observe *Samuel Relating to Eli the Judgements of God upon Eli's House* by John Singleton Copley. Play Hide & Describe.

Recite Recite Jeremiah 29:12-13.

Pray Tell God you want to grow in your relationship with Him by talking to Him more.

Tell God you trust Him with your worries and anxieties and to replace them with truth and peace. *If your child hasn't prayed aloud before, this week would be a great time to encourage and practice.*

Bible Notebook

Practice prayer journaling by writing a prayer to God in your Bible Notebook and illustrating it.

DAY 2

Declare Say "I will talk to God and He talks to me" three times.

Sing Sing the hymn "All the Way My Savior Leads Me" and follow along with the lyrics sheet.

Read Read Matthew 6:5-13.

Having a consistent prayer life is foundational to a relationship with God. It connects us and puts us in a position to receive encouragement and instruction from God. In this passage, Jesus is teaching His followers key points on how to pray.

Discuss What point was Jesus trying to make about praying in public versus in secret?

Discuss the main points of the Lord's Prayer and locate them in the passage: praising God, asking for His kingdom to come on earth, praying for provision, forgiveness, guidance, and protection.

Beauty Read "I Heard the Voice of Jesus Say" by John B. Dykes.
Discuss any unknown vocabulary and meanings.

Recite Recite Jeremiah 29:12-13.

Pray Thank God for "The Lord's Prayer" that guides us on how to pray. Tell God you desire to know Him more and want to grow your prayer life.

Practice "The Lord's Prayer" in your own words.

Dig Deeper

Study what "give us this day our daily bread" means beyond physical provision. Could Jesus have meant more than praying for actual food? Read John 6:31-59 and discuss.

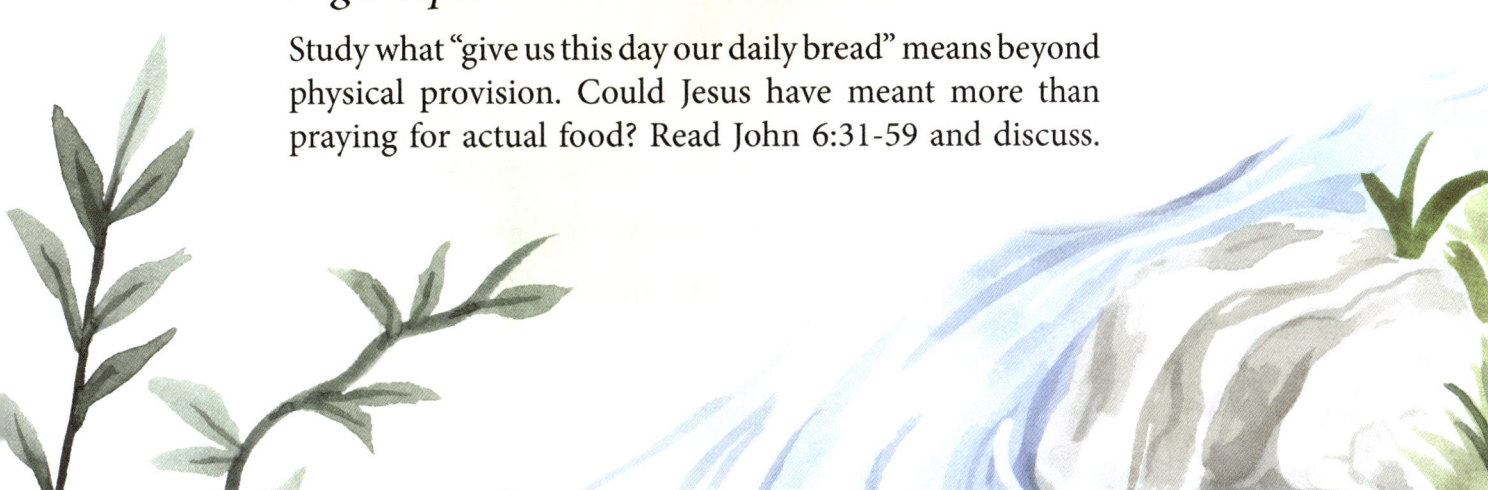

DAY 3

Declare — Say "I will talk to God and He talks to me" three times.

Sing — Sing the hymn "All the Way My Savior Leads Me" and follow along with the lyrics sheet.

Read — Read 1 Samuel 3:1-10.

In the Old Testament, followers of God didn't have access to the Holy Spirit to guide them like we do today. Instead, God sometimes spoke audibly or through manifestations (e.g. the burning bush). In this story, Samuel heard the voice of God out loud.

Discuss — Once Samuel realized he was hearing God's voice, how did he respond?

Recall other ways and times God spoke to followers in the Old Testament.

Discuss the various ways God speaks to us today.

Beauty — Observe *Samuel Relating to Eli the Judgements of God upon Eli's House* by John Singleton Copley. What emotions do you think Samuel and Eli feel in the moment depicted?

Recite — Recite Jeremiah 29:12-13.

Pray — Thank God for giving us the Holy Spirit to guide us.

Ask God for the courage to respond as Samuel did when God spoke to him.

Bible Notebook

Write a summary of the story you read today and draw a picture to represent it.

DAY 4

Declare — Say "I will talk to God and He talks to me" three times.

Sing — Sing the hymn "All the Way My Savior Leads Me" and follow along with the lyrics sheet.

Read — Read John 16:5-15.

After Jesus was crucified and raised to life, the Holy Spirit came to dwell in the disciples. When you receive Christ, you also get the Holy Spirit in you as your helper and counselor. It takes practice to recognize the still, small voice of the Holy Spirit.

Discuss — Share a time you felt the Holy Spirit speaking or guiding you. Explain how and what you heard and what it felt like.

Discuss the roles of the Holy Spirit—it provides encouragement, comfort, instruction, conviction, guidance, and more.

Beauty — Read "I Heard the Voice of Jesus Say" by John B. Dykes.
Recite any portions from memory or copy your favorite stanza.

Recite — Recite Jeremiah 29:12-13.

Pray — Thank God for the Holy Spirit dwelling inside you. Tell God you want to tune your heart to hear His voice more clearly.

Ask God for guidance or comfort for something specific in your life right now.

Family Connection

Be still and practice hearing the Holy Spirit. Begin by asking God to speak. Play soft music and if anyone senses anything, invite them to write it down or draw a picture. Share and discuss.

DAY 5

Declare Say "I will talk to God and He talks to me" three times.

Sing Sing the hymn "All the Way My Savior Leads Me" and follow along with the lyrics sheet.

Read Read John 10:1-30.

In this passage, Jesus calls His followers the sheep and Himself the shepherd. The sheep know and follow His voice. The shepherd brings safety, provision, and guidance. In the same way, the more we recognize and follow Jesus' voice, the more abundant life we will live with Him. God never calls us to do something sinful or that contradicts what He has said in His word.

Discuss Discuss how God desires to guide us—not to control us, but instead to invite us into a life with Him.

Contrast what the enemy has planned for us versus what God has planned for us.

Talk about lies the enemy has tried to plant in your mind and heart. How did you combat them?

Beauty Replicate a portion or all of this week's artwork or draw or paint what you imagine when you read this week's poem.

Recite Recite Jeremiah 29:12-13.

Pray Thank Jesus for being a good leader and shepherd. Ask Jesus to help you discern his voice from the enemy's voice.

Play

Designate one child to be the "sheep" and blindfold them. Lead them through obstacles on the floor with your voice. Meanwhile, other family members can shout wrong directions or play loud background noise, but the "sheep" must focus on your voice to lead them.

Devotion:
I will trust God, even when I don't understand.

Declaration:	I will trust God, even when I don't understand.
Song:	"Great is Thy Faithfulness"
Verse:	Proverbs 3:5-6
Poem:	"The Lord Will Provide" by John Newton
Artwork:	*Paul and Silas Leaving the Prison in Philippi* by Nicolas de Plattemontagne

Trust in the Lord with all your heart, and lean not on your own understanding. In all your ways acknowledge him, and he will make straight your paths.

Proverbs 3:5-6

Devotion: I will trust God, even when I don't understand.

Great is Thy Faithfulness

Great is Thy faithfulness
O God my Father
There is no shadow
Of turning with Thee
Thou changest not
Thy compassions they fail not
As Thou hast been
Thou forever will be

Great is Thy faithfulness
Great is Thy faithfulness
Morning by morning
New mercies I see
All I have needed
Thy hand hath provided
Great is Thy faithfulness
Lord unto me

Summer and winter
Springtime and harvest
Sun moon and stars
In their courses above
Join with all nature
In manifold witness
To Thy great faithfulness
Mercy and love

Great is Thy faithfulness
Great is Thy faithfulness
Morning by morning
New mercies I see
All I have needed
Thy hand hath provided
Great is Thy faithfulness
Lord unto me

Pardon for sin
And a peace that endureth
Thine own dear presence
To cheer and to guide
Strength for today
And bright hope for tomorrow
Blessings all mine
With ten thousand beside

Great is Thy faithfulness
Great is Thy faithfulness
Morning by morning
New mercies I see
All I have needed
Thy hand hath provided
Great is Thy faithfulness
Great is Thy faithfulness
Great is Thy faithfulness
Lord unto thee

Though troubles assail us
And dangers affright,
Though friends should all fail us
And foes all unite—
Yet one thing secures us,
Whatever betide,
The promise assures us:
"The Lord will provide."

The birds, without garner
Or storehouse are fed;
From them let us learn
To trust God for our bread.
His saints what is fitting
Shall ne'er be denied,
So long as 'tis written,
"The Lord will provide."

God's call we obey
Like Abram of old,
Not knowing our way;
But faith makes us bold,
For though we are strangers,
We have a good Guide,
And trust through all dangers,
"The Lord will provide."

When Satan assails us
To stop up our path,
And courage all fails us—
We triumph by faith.
He cannot take from us
(Though oft he has tried)
This heart-cheering promise,
"The Lord will provide."

He tells us we're weak,
Our hope is in vain,
The good that we seek
We ne'er shall obtain;
But when such suggestions
Our graces have tried,
This answers all questions—
"The Lord will provide."

No strength of our own
And no goodness we claim;
Yet, since we have known
Of the Savior's great Name,
In this our strong tower
For safety we hide:
The Lord is our power,
"The Lord will provide."

When life sinks apace,
And death is in view,
The word of His grace
Shall comfort us through;
Not fearing or doubting,
With Christ on our side,
We hope to die shouting,
"The Lord will provide!"

*"The Lord Will Provide"
by John Newton*

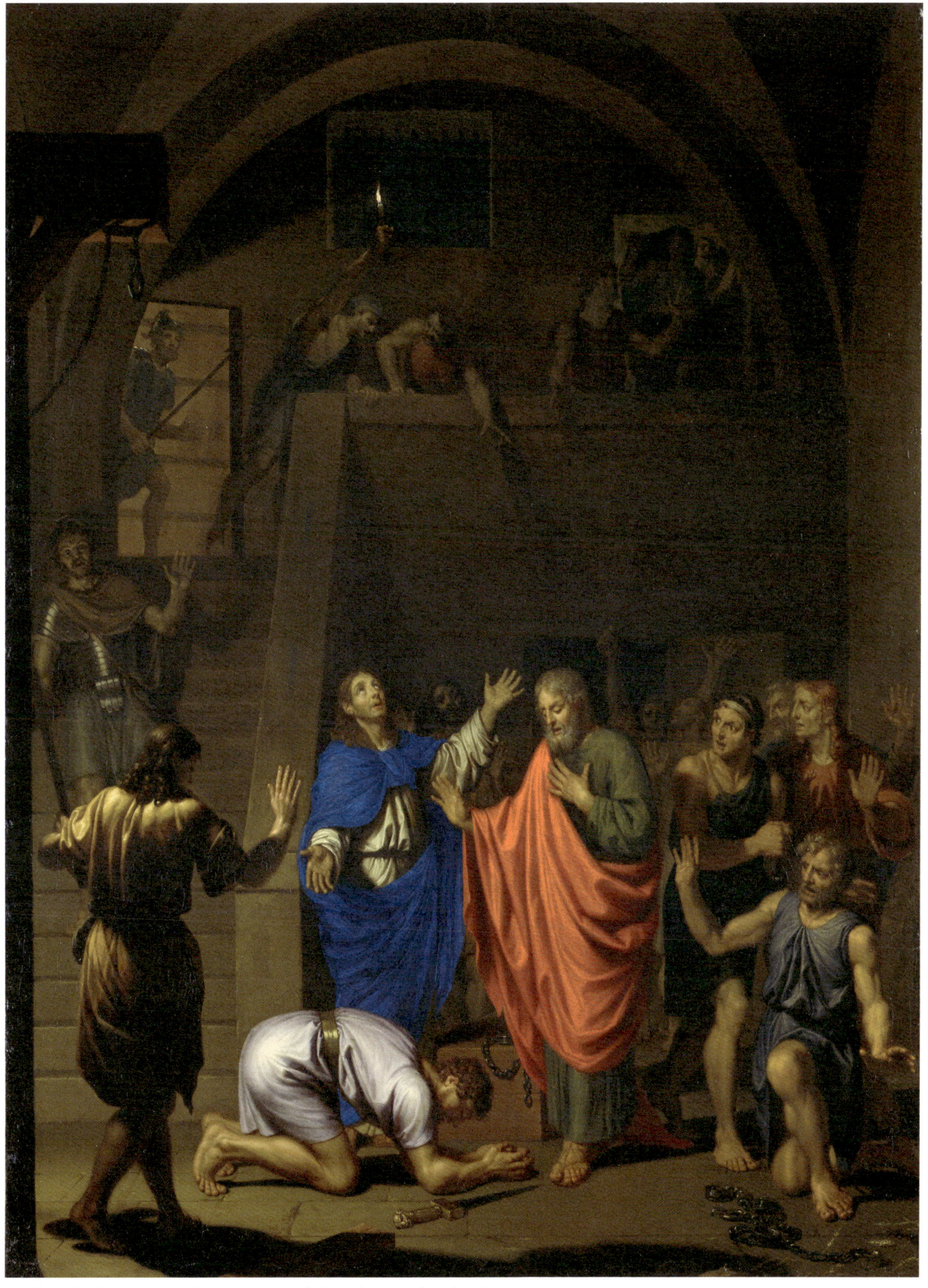

Devotion: I will trust God, even when I don't understand.

Paul and Silas Leaving the Prison in Philippi by Nicolas de Plattemontagne
ca. 1665-66

DAY 1

Declare — Say "I will trust God, even when I don't understand" three times.

Sing — Sing the hymn "Great is Thy Faithfulness" and follow along with the lyrics sheet.

Read — Read Jeremiah 17:5-8 & Psalm 1:1-3.

When our roots are deep and we draw from the Living Water (Jesus), we will be strong. We will thrive and bear fruit, even in hard times. When we place our hope and trust in anything other than God, we set ourselves up for destruction in difficult times.

Discuss — Tell a story about a time that you went through something difficult. Did you feel like a bush in the wasteland or the firmly rooted tree?

What are some characteristics and fruits of a person who lives planted by the streams of Living Water?

What can you do daily to position yourself to be like a tree by the water?

Beauty — Observe *Paul and Silas Leaving the Prison in Philippi* by Nicolas de Plattemontagne. Play Hide & Describe.

Recite — Recite Proverbs 3:5-6.

Pray — Tell God your confidence and trust are in Him alone. Thank God for giving us a way to prepare for hard times in life. Ask God to help you with daily disciplines that will root you in Him.

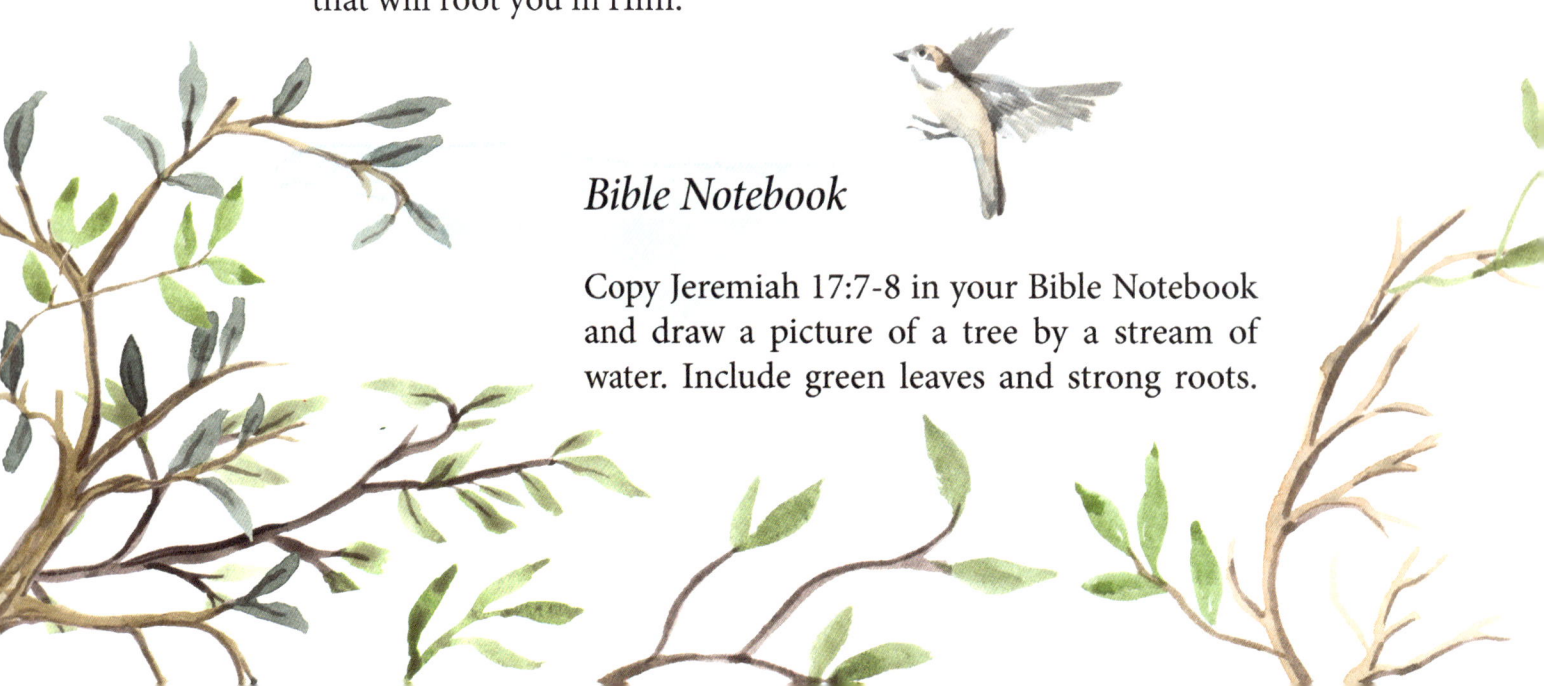

Bible Notebook

Copy Jeremiah 17:7-8 in your Bible Notebook and draw a picture of a tree by a stream of water. Include green leaves and strong roots.

DAY 2

Declare   Say "I will trust God, even when I don't understand" three times.

Sing   Sing the hymn "Great is Thy Faithfulness" and follow along with the lyrics sheet.

Read   Read Psalm 143:1-12 and Psalm 119:88-90.

David wrote Psalm 143 when he was in crisis. He was running for his life from his enemies, yet he continued to trust God. He remembered God's faithfulness in the past, even though things seemed hopeless. One way we can stay deeply rooted in our faith is to recall ways God has been faithful over many generations and in our lives.

Discuss   Share stories about God's faithfulness in your life or others in your family.

Find verses in the psalm that show David remembering God's faithfulness and telling God he trusts Him.

What are some stories from the Old Testament that David could have been recalling that display God's faithfulness?

Beauty   Read "The Lord Will Provide" by John Newton. Discuss any unknown vocabulary and meanings.

Recite   Recite Proverbs 3:5-6.

Pray   Thank God for specific ways He has been faithful to you and those who have gone before you.

Ask God to help you recall His faithfulness in hard times.

Poet Study

Do an internet study on John Newton, the author of this week's poem. Listen to the hymn version in the Spotify playlist. What difficulties did Newton go through that may have inspired this piece?

DAY 3

Declare Say "I will trust God, even when I don't understand" three times.

Sing Sing the hymn "Great is Thy Faithfulness" and follow along with the lyrics sheet.

Read Read Acts 16:16-40.

Paul and Silas are incredible examples of trusting God no matter what. In this story, they have been beaten and thrown into prison. Rather than questioning God and grumbling, they worshipped God and shared the gospel. Their display of trust in God became an open door to others becoming believers and followers of Jesus.

Discuss Why did Paul and Silas get thrown into jail? Discuss persecution around the world today.

Paul and Silas could have immediately escaped during the earthquake, but they didn't. Why not?

How did Paul and Silas's trust in God affect others? How can yours?

Beauty Observe *Paul and Silas Leaving the Prison in Philippi* by Nicolas de Plattemontagne. What do you notice about the colors in this painting?

Recite Recite Proverbs 3:5-6.

Pray Thank God for examples in the Bible of people who trusted Him in challenging circumstances. Ask God to give you the courage to trust and glorify Him no matter what. Pray for the persecuted church today.

Bible Notebook

In your Bible Notebook, summarize the ways Paul and Silas trusted God. Illustrate what you wrote.

DAY 4

Declare Say "I will trust God, even when I don't understand" three times.

Sing Sing the hymn "Great is Thy Faithfulness" and follow along with the lyrics sheet.

Read Read Psalm 136.

This psalm, written by David, was given to the Levites to sing every day to remind them of God's faithfulness (1 Chronicles 16). It specifically thanks God for the ways He showed His glory to the Israelites and delivered them. By recalling God's faithfulness daily, they were able to persevere in trusting God in hard times.

Discuss Go through the psalm and discuss what Bible stories each section refers to.

If you were writing a psalm, what testimonies and praises would you include from your personal life or family line?

Why do you think the psalm repeats the phrase "His steadfast love endures forever"?

Beauty Read "The Lord Will Provide" by John Newton. Recite any portions from memory or copy your favorite stanza.

Recite Recite Proverbs 3:5-6.

Pray Thank God for His steadfast love that has pursued humankind throughout history. Thank God for the Bible and its stories and reminders of God's faithfulness.

Creative Writing

Write your own psalm using the same format as Psalm 136. Declare something God has done for you, and on the next line write, "Your steadfast love endures forever."

DAY 5

Declare	Say "I will trust God, even when I don't understand" three times.
Sing	Sing the hymn "Great is Thy Faithfulness" and follow along with the lyrics sheet.
Read	Read Genesis 6:5-9:17.
	Noah is a great example of a man who trusted God even when others thought he was crazy. Noah didn't see any rain coming, but he built the ark anyway. Noah's commitment to obey God saved his family and the generations after. It is imperative to obey God at all costs, even when we don't see the full picture.
Discuss	How do trusting God and obedience go hand-in-hand?
	How do you think Noah felt when he started building the ark? How about when the rain started to pour?
	Have you ever felt different than your peers because of your choice to obey God?
Beauty	Replicate a portion or all of this week's artwork or draw or paint what you imagine when you read this week's poem.
Recite	Recite Proverbs 3:5-6.
Pray	Ask God to give you the courage to make the right choices, even among others who live differently. Thank God for being trustworthy and keeping His promises.

Bible Notebook

Watercolor or draw a rainbow to remind you that God keeps His promises. Copy Psalm 119:90 on the lines. Listen to the song "Your Faithfulness" from Jon Thurlow (in Spotify playlist) while you create.

Wisdom:
I will walk on the path of life.

Declaration: I will walk on the path of life.

Song: "The Perfect Wisdom of Our God"

Verse: Proverbs 4:11-13

Poem: "Fight the Good Fight" by J. S. B. Monsell

Artwork: *The Court of King Solomon* by Nikolai Ge

*I have taught you the way of wisdom;
I have led you in the paths of uprightness.
When you walk, your step
will not be hampered,
and if you run, you will not stumble.
Keep hold of instruction; do not let go;
guard her, for she is your life.*

Proverbs 4:11-13

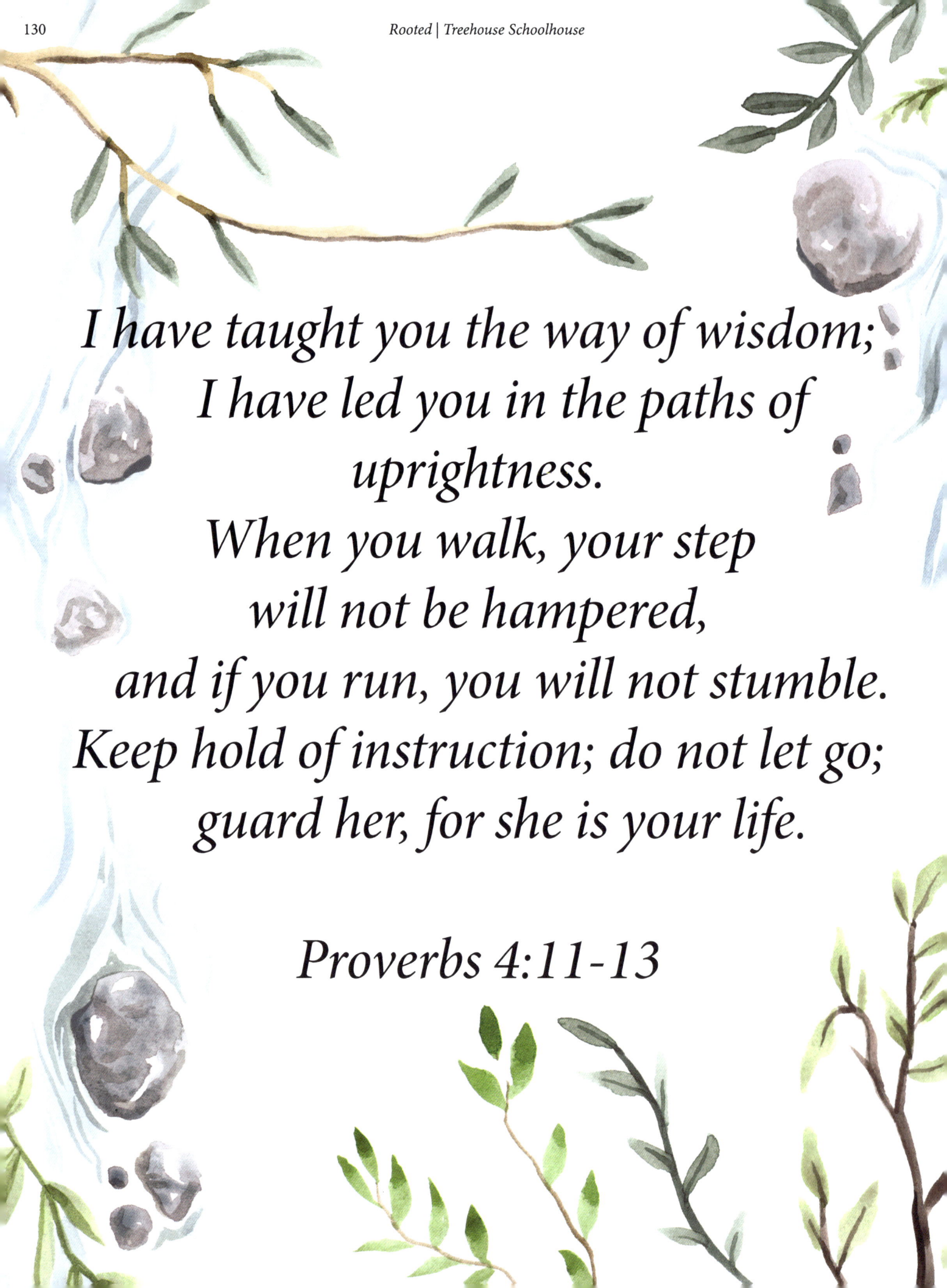

The Perfect Wisdom of Our God

The perfect wisdom of our God
Revealed in all the universe
All things created by His hand
And held together at His command

He knows the mysteries of the seas
The secrets of the stars are His
He guides the planets on their way
And turns the earth through another day

The matchless wisdom of His ways
That mark the path of righteousness
His Word a lamp unto my feet
His Spirit teaching and guiding me

And oh, the mystery of the cross
That God should suffer for the lost
So that the fool might shame the wise
And all the glory might go to Christ

Oh, grant me wisdom from above
To pray for peace and cling to love
And teach me humbly to receive
The sun and rain of Your sovereignty

Each strand of sorrow has a place
Within this tapestry of grace
So through the trials I choose to say
"Your perfect will in Your perfect way"

Fight the good fight with all thy might;
Christ is thy strength, and Christ thy right.
Lay hold on life, and it shall be
Thy joy and crown eternally.

Run the straight race through God's good grace,
Lift up thine eyes, and seek His Face.
Life with its way before thee lies;
Christ is the path, and Christ thy prize.

Cast care aside, lean on thy Guide,
His boundless mercy will provide.
Lean, and the trusting soul shall prove,
Christ is its life, and Christ its love.

Faint not, nor fear. His arms are near;
He changeth not, and thou art dear.
Only believe, and thou shalt see
That Christ is all in all to thee.

"Fight the Good Fight"
by J. S. B. Monsell

Wisdom: I will walk on the path of life.

The Court of King Solomon by Nikolai Ge
ca. 1854

DAY 1

Declare — Say "I will walk on the path of life" three times.

Sing — Sing the hymn "The Perfect Wisdom of Our God" and follow along with the lyrics sheet.

Read — Read 1 Kings 3:5-12, 1 Kings 4:29-31, and James 1:5.

God called Solomon to do a big job at a young age. Solomon could have asked God for material possessions. Instead, Solomon asked for God's wisdom on living and being a good king. When we pray for wisdom in living our lives and following His instructions, we actively choose to walk on the path of life.

Discuss — What is the most challenging part about being a king? Would you like to be one?

Talk about a time you walked on a path. How did you know the right ways to go?

Discuss how the world promotes false wisdom and how we find true wisdom.

Beauty — Observe *The Court of King Solomon* by Nikolai Ge.
Play Hide & Describe.

Recite — Recite Proverbs 4:11-13.

Pray — Tell God you desire His wisdom over the world's wisdom.

Ask God to help you to respond to Him and to seek His word and voice for navigating life.

Thank God for being generous and ready to answer when we ask for wisdom.

Dig Deeper

Read and discuss 1 Kings 3:16-28. This story shows a time Solomon used God's wisdom to handle a difficult situation as king.

DAY 2

Declare Say "I will walk on the path of life" three times.

Sing Sing the hymn "The Perfect Wisdom of Our God" and follow along with the lyrics sheet.

Read Read Proverbs 1:1-7 and Proverbs 2.

Proverbs was written by King Solomon. It is a book filled with wisdom and direction on staying on the path of life. Wisdom is a valuable treasure we should always seek. The beginning of finding wisdom is to "fear God." When you live your life with wisdom, it brings many benefits.

Discuss Discuss what it means to fear God. What does that look like in your life?

Revisit Proverbs 2 and identify the benefits of living a life of wisdom.

Discuss the meaning of the language "forbidden woman" and "adulteress" literally and figuratively.

Beauty Read "Fight the Good Fight" by J. S. B. Monsell.
Discuss any unknown vocabulary and meanings.

Recite Recite Proverbs 4:11-13.

Pray Thank God for giving us the book of Proverbs to learn from.

Confess any sin that you need to admit—anything that is pulling you away from your walk with God.

Ask God for vigilance so you can be on guard from anything that could lead you away.

Create

Watercolor a picture of two paths—one leading to lush, green pastures and the other to darkness. Copy Psalm 16:11 somewhere on the page.

DAY 3

Declare   Say "I will walk on the path of life" three times.

Sing   Sing the hymn "The Perfect Wisdom of Our God" and follow along with the lyrics sheet.

Read   Read Matthew 7:24-27.

Jesus was teaching a crowd of people many things about life and the kingdom of God. At the end of the sermon, He ends the message with this story of the wise vs. the foolish man. It illustrates what a life built on truth looks like compared to a life built on foolish, meaningless things.

Discuss   What was Jesus teaching the people before he shared this story? (Refer to the Sermon on the Mount, Matthew 5-7.)

Talk about how a house is built and how important the foundation is.

What kinds of things does a wise person do and pursue in life? What about a foolish person?

Beauty   Observe *The Court of King Solomon* by Nikolai Ge. What Bible story is this depicting (1 Kings 3:16-28)? What emotions do you think the people are feeling?

Recite   Recite Proverbs 4:11-13.

Pray   Ask God for wisdom for anything specific in your life that you need guidance on.

Ask God to give you love and hunger for His word, so that you may always seek truth and wisdom from it.

Pray for anyone who comes to mind, that they may choose to walk on the path of life.

Bible Notebook

Write a summary of the story you read today and draw a picture to represent it.

DAY 4

Declare   Say "I will walk on the path of life" three times.

Sing   Sing the hymn "The Perfect Wisdom of Our God" and follow along with the lyrics sheet.

Read   Read Proverbs 3.

This proverb is full of wisdom that instructs us how to live. Notice in verses 1-12 the amount of "cause and effect" statements that Solomon teaches. Living a life of wisdom is more precious than gold—and it is available for everyone. Finding and walking in wisdom requires something from us. It requires a life dedicated to seeking God and continually choosing to walk on the path of life.

Discuss   What does it mean to "bind them around your neck and write them on the tablet of your heart" (verse 3)?

Discuss the difference between being knowledgeable and having wisdom.

Discuss how to practically live a life that seeks out wisdom (studying the Bible, fellowship with other believers, seeking wise counsel, prayer, etc.).

Beauty   Read "Fight the Good Fight" by J. S. B. Monsell.
Recite any portions from memory or copy your favorite stanza.

Recite   Recite Proverbs 4:11-13.

Pray   Tell God how much you value His wisdom and that you will seek it like a treasure.

Thank God for any relationships that offer you wise counsel or encourage you to walk on the path of life.

Pray through Proverbs 3 and thank God for the benefits He offers when we live a life of wisdom.

Demonstrate

Hide "treasures" for your children to find (coins, candy, etc.). As they hunt for the treasure, say "wisdom" they get near it and "folly" as they move further away.

DAY 5

Declare	Say "I will walk on the path of life" three times.
Sing	Sing the hymn "The Perfect Wisdom of Our God" and follow along with the lyrics sheet.
Read	Read Proverbs 4.
	In this proverb, Solomon is instructing his son in wisdom. God puts people of authority in our lives to help guide us in wisdom. Two important keys to staying on the path of life are intentionally valuing wisdom and avoiding the path of the wicked. If you know what each path looks like, it will be easier to stay on the right one.
Discuss	Talk about a time a trusted person in authority gave you the direction or counsel you needed.
	Discuss the differences between the path of the righteous and the path of the wicked according to this passage.
	What does it mean to "keep your heart with all vigilance" in verse 23? How can you do that?
Beauty	Replicate a portion or all of this week's artwork or draw or paint what you imagine when you read this week's poem.
Recite	Recite Proverbs 4:11-13.
Pray	Thank God for the people in your life who help guide you in wisdom and truth.
	Ask God to protect you from the path of wickedness and people who would pull you astray.
	Tell God you will choose to stay on the path of life and righteousness.

Bible Notebook

Draw a picture of yourself with a crown or garland on your head. Copy Proverbs 4:7-9 on the lines.

Wisdom:
I will honor my parents and authorities.

Declaration: I will honor my parents and authorities.

Song: "Children and Fathers (Ephesians 6:1-4)"

Verse: Ephesians 6:1-3

Poem: "Let Children Hear the Mighty Deeds" by Isaac Watts

Artwork: *Nehemiah before King Artaxerxes, initial 'C' from a Bible* by Masters of Zweder van Culemborg

Children, obey your parents in the Lord, for this is right. "Honor your father and mother" (this is the first commandment with a promise), "that it may go well with you and that you may live long in the land."

Ephesians 6:1-3

Children and Fathers (Ephesians 6:1-4)

Children, obey your parents in the Lord, for this is right
Children, obey your parents in the Lord, for this is right
Honor your father and your mother
This is the first commandment
Honor your father and your mother
This is the first commandment
With a promise, oh Lord

Children, obey your parents in the Lord, for this is right
Children, obey your parents in the Lord, for this is right
That it may go well with you and that you may live long in the land

Now fathers, do not provoke your children to anger
I said, fathers, do not provoke your children to anger
But bring them up in the discipline
and instruction of the Lord
Bring them up in the discipline
and instruction of the Lord

Fathers, do not provoke your children to anger
Children, obey your parents in the Lord
I said, fathers, do not provoke your children to anger
And children, obey your parents in the Lord
For this is right, you know it's right
Yeah this is right, you know it's right

Let children hear the mighty deeds
which God performed of old;
which in our younger years we saw,
and which our fathers told.

He bids us make his glories known,
his works of pow'r and grace;
and we'll convey his wonders down
through ev'ry rising race.

Our lips shall tell them to our sons,
and they again to theirs;
that generations yet unborn
may teach them to their heirs.

Thus shall they learn in God alone
their hope securely stands,
that they may ne'er forget his works,
but practice his commands.

"Let Children Hear the Mighty Deeds"
by Isaac Watts

Wisdom: I will honor my parents and authorities. 143

Nehemiah before King Artaxerxes, initial 'C' from a Bible by Masters of Zweder van Culemborg ca. 1415-1440

DAY 1

Declare Say "I will honor my parents and authorities" three times.

Sing Sing the song "Children and Fathers (Ephesians 6:1-4)" and follow along with the lyrics sheet.

Read Read Hebrews 13:7, 17 and Titus 3:1.

Often God appoints authorities in our lives who aren't our parents, but we are called to honor them. These passages remind us to look to our godly leaders and let them be an example of how we live our lives. We should be thankful for their leadership and follow their guidance in joy.

Discuss What authorities in your life do you regularly submit to? What is their role in your life?

Discuss how to know which authorities and/or situations children should obey and which they shouldn't. How can they discern the difference?

What would it be like if you never obeyed any authority? What would the consequences be?

Beauty Observe *Nehemiah before King Artaxerxes, initial 'C' from a Bible* by Masters of Zweder van Culemborg. Play Hide & Describe.

Recite Recite Ephesians 6:1-3.

Pray Thank God specifically for the authorities in your life that He has given you and how they teach and guide you.

Ask God to help you honor the authorities in your life.

Ask God to prepare you for kingdom work, even now as a child.

Create

Make a gift or card for an authority in your life. Thank them for investing in you. Mail or deliver the gift to them.

DAY 2

Declare — Say "I will honor my parents and authorities" three times.

Sing — Sing the song "Children and Fathers (Ephesians 6:1-4)" and follow along with the lyrics sheet.

Read — Read 1 Timothy 2:1-4.

As followers of Jesus, we are called to pray for our leaders. In this passage, it references kings, but today we have different authorities such as governors and presidents. First and foremost, we should pray for the salvation of our leaders. We should also pray God's will be done on earth as it is in heaven under their leadership.

Discuss — What is the difference between supplications, intercessions, and thanksgiving?

Discuss your governor and your president and what you know about their beliefs.

Discuss any local, state, and/or national current events that your family could pray about.

Beauty — Read "Let Children Hear the Mighty Deeds" by Isaac Watts.
Discuss any unknown vocabulary and meanings.

Recite — Recite Ephesians 6:1-3.

Pray — Thank God for being the ultimate authority and for placing men and women in government positions.

Pray specifically for a local, national, or global current event. Pray for an upcoming election or specific leader in government.

Bible Notebook

Write down a prayer for a specific leader in government or your life in your Bible Notebook. Draw a picture of the leader in the blank space.

DAY 3

Declare Say "I will honor my parents and authorities" three times.

Sing Sing the song "Children and Fathers (Ephesians 6:1-4)" and follow along with the lyrics sheet.

Read Read Nehemiah 1-2:8.

Nehemiah was in captivity as the cupbearer to King Artaxerxes. While he was there, his people, the Israelites, were in exile. The wall around Jerusalem had been destroyed and he wanted to return and rebuild it. He submitted to the king's leadership in an honorable way and asked for permission to go. God blessed Nehemiah for seeking Him first and honoring His earthly authority. He made a way for him to go and rebuild the wall.

Discuss What does it mean to be in captivity? What does it mean that the Israelites were in exile?

How do you think Nehemiah felt coming to the king with such a great request? What gave him the courage?

Discuss how you could be in a similar situation as Nehemiah in today—needing permission from an earthly authority to do kingdom work.

Beauty Observe *Nehemiah before King Artaxerxes, initial 'C' from a Bible* by Masters of Zweder van Culemborg.
What do you think the people are thinking and feeling in this picture?

Recite Recite Ephesians 6:1-3.

Pray Ask God to give you the boldness to do kingdom work, no matter what circumstance you find yourself in.

Pray for any leaders in your life who don't follow Jesus. Pray for their salvation and that they would come to know God and lead people in His ways.

Bible Notebook

Write a summary of the story you read today and draw a picture to represent it.

DAY 4

Declare — Say "I will honor my parents and authorities" three times.

Sing — Sing the song "Children and Fathers (Ephesians 6:1-4)" and follow along with the lyrics sheet.

Read — Read Ephesians 6:1-3.

Paul wrote Ephesians and is reminding the church of the fifth commandment. To honor means to highly respect and esteem someone. Obeying our parents is the best way to honor them. To obey "in the Lord" means to obey with our actions, but also with our hearts.

Discuss — What does it mean to "obey with our hearts"?

Have you ever felt honored? How do you treat someone you highly esteem?

Imagine if there was no parent or authority as a leader. What would that look like in your home?

Beauty — Read "Let Children Hear the Mighty Deeds" by Isaac Watts.
Recite any portions from memory or copy your favorite stanza.

Recite — Recite Ephesians 6:1-3.

Pray — Thank God for giving you parents who love and lead you.

Ask God to forgive you for the ways you haven't honored your parents in your actions or your heart.

Ask God to help you show respect and honor to your parents today.

Family Connection

Think of simple and specific ways you can show your parents love and honor by serving them. Write the ideas down on slips of paper and let your parents randomly select one for you to do now. Allow them to choose several or save the other slips for another day.

DAY 5

Declare Say "I will honor my parents and authorities" three times.

Sing Sing the song "Children and Fathers (Ephesians 6:1-4)" and follow along with the lyrics sheet.

Read Read Proverbs 6:20-23.

Solomon was instructing his son to hold tightly to the guidance given by his mother and father. Solomon tells his son to bind them to his heart and tie them around his neck, which means to hold their instructions in his heart wherever he goes. Everywhere you go, your parent's guidance can stay close to your heart to help you make the right choices.

Discuss Talk about a time you were tempted to do something you shouldn't and there wasn't a person in authority there to guide you. Did you think of their instructions at that moment? What did you do?

What are some specific instructions that your parents have given you that you hold close to your heart everywhere you go?

Beauty Replicate a portion or all of this week's artwork or draw or paint what you imagine when you read this week's poem.

Recite Recite Ephesians 6:1-3.

Pray Thank God specifically for each of your parents and for all they do to guide you into truth.

Ask God to help you recall the wisdom and instruction of your leaders in times that you need it.

Dig Deeper

Look up Exodus 13:1-16 and Deuteronomy 6:4-9. Research how the Israelites would fasten scripture to their arms and heads as a sign they were keeping them close to their minds and hearts.

Wisdom:
I will take my thoughts captive and think on true things.

Declaration: I will take my thoughts captive and think on true things.

Hymn: "Turn Your Eyes Upon Jesus"

Verse: Philippians 4:6

Poem: "In the Secret of His Presence" by Ellen Lakshmi Goreh

Artwork: *The Thinker* by Auguste Rodin

Do not be anxious about anything, but in everything by prayer and supplication with thanksgiving let your requests be made known to God.

Philippians 4:6

Turn Your Eyes Upon Jesus

Turn your eyes upon Jesus
Look full in His wonderful face
And the things of earth will grow strangely dim
In the light of His glory and grace

O soul, are you weary and troubled?
No light in the darkness you see?
There's light for a look at the Savior
And life more abundant and free

Through death into life everlasting
He passed and we follow Him there
O'er us sin no more hath dominion
For more than conquerors we are

Oh, turn your eyes upon Jesus
Look full in His wonderful face
And the things of earth will grow strangely dim
In the light of His glory and grace

His word shall not fail you, He promised
Believe Him and all will be well
Then go to a world that is dying
His perfect salvation to tell

Oh, turn your eyes upon Jesus
Look full in His wonderful face
And the things of earth will grow strangely dim
In the light of His glory and grace

Oh, turn your, oh, turn your
Oh, turn your eyes upon Jesus
(repeat)

In the secret of His presence
How my soul delights to hide!
Oh, how precious are the lessons
Which I learn at Jesus' side!
Earthly cares can never vex me,
Neither trials lay me low;
For when Satan comes to tempt me,
To the secret place I go,
To the secret place I go.

When my soul is faint and thirsty,
'Neath the shadow of His wing
There is cool and pleasant shelter,
And a fresh and crystal spring;
And my Savior rests beside me,
As we hold communion sweet;
If I tried, I could not utter
What He says when thus we meet,
What He says when thus we meet.

Excerpt from "In the Secret of His Presence"
by Ellen Lakshmi Goreh

Wisdom: I will take my thoughts captive and think on true things.

The Thinker by Auguste Rodin
ca. 1879-1889

DAY 1

Declare	Say "I will take my thoughts captive and think on true things" three times.
Sing	Sing the hymn "Turn Your Eyes Upon Jesus" and follow along with the lyrics sheet.
Read	Read 2 Corinthians 10:3-6.
	There is a spiritual battle happening, even though we can't see it. When thoughts come into our minds that are untrue and destructive, we can fight them with the weapons that God has given us. You are the only person who can fight against your negative thoughts. You have to learn to do it yourself.
Discuss	What are examples of thoughts against the truth that could come into our minds?
	What weapons can we use to fight these thoughts? (The Bible, worship, replacing lies with truth.)
	Talk about a lie you believed and share how you replaced it with the truth.
Beauty	Observe *The Thinker* by Auguste Rodin. Play Hide & Describe.
Recite	Recite Philippians 4:6.
Pray	Thank God for giving us the Bible to combat the lies that come into our minds.
	Ask God to help you stay alert against the attacks of the enemy.
	Confess a lie you have believed and tell God you want to dwell on the truth instead.

Dig Deeper

Identify one lie you often have in your mind. Find a scripture that tells the truth about that lie. Write it down on an index card or slip of paper and tape it somewhere that you see often to remind you of the truth.

DAY 2

Declare	Say "I will take my thoughts captive and think on true things" three times.
Sing	Sing the hymn "Turn Your Eyes Upon Jesus" and follow along with the lyrics sheet.
Read	Read Psalm 139:23-24 and Matthew 6:25-34.
	Anxiety and worry can overtake our minds if we don't stay vigilant and take our thoughts captive. Sometimes when we feel unsettled in our hearts, we don't even know why. Like David in this psalm, we can come to God and ask Him to search our hearts. If we can identify our worries, it will be easier to bring them to God.
Discuss	What are some things you worry about often?
	Talk about a time you felt anxious but couldn't identify why. How did you move forward from there?
	What is the solution to stop worrying about our needs being met? (See Matthew 6:33.)
Beauty	Read "In the Secret of His Presence" by Ellen Lakshmi Goreh. Discuss any unknown vocabulary and meanings.
Recite	Recite Philippians 4:6.
Pray	Thank God for being a trustworthy provider.
	Thank God for helping you identify worries and anxieties.
	Ask God to protect your heart and mind and help you stay alert against lies.

Family Connection

Play calming music or a worship playlist and ask God to bring up anything causing anxiety or worry. Children can write down what they feel or draw a picture. Take turns sharing and praying for each other.

DAY 3

Declare — Say "I will take my thoughts captive and think on true things" three times.

Sing — Sing the hymn "Turn Your Eyes Upon Jesus" and follow along with the lyrics sheet.

Read — Read Romans 12:2 and Philippians 4:8.

As followers of God, we are called to be different from the world—including how we think. Renewing our minds looks like kicking out all thoughts that are against the truth and, instead, thinking about things that are true, honorable, just, pure, lovely, commendable, excellent, and worthy of praise.

Discuss — Discuss the meaning of each type of thought in Philippians 4:8. Share examples of what those thoughts could be.

Discuss examples of thoughts that would be against the truth and opposite to the qualities mentioned in Philippians 4:8.

What does it mean to test and approve the will of God in Romans 12:2?

Beauty — Observe *The Thinker* by Auguste Rodin.
What do you think *The Thinker* is pondering based on his body language?

Recite — Recite Philippians 4:6.

Pray — Ask God to forgive you for times you have dwelled on thoughts against His desires.

Tell God you want to be different from the world and renew your mind.

Tell God that you want to know His will for your life.

Artist Study

Do an artist study of the French sculptor, Auguste Rodin. Learn more about the creation of *The Thinker* and research other sculptures he created. Locate France on a map or globe.

DAY 4

Declare   Say "I will take my thoughts captive and think on true things" three times.

Sing   Sing the hymn "Turn Your Eyes Upon Jesus" and follow along with the lyrics sheet.

Read   Read Ephesians 6:10-20 and Hebrews 4:12.

As believers, we have protection against the attacks of the enemy. These attacks often begin in our minds. The Bible calls these tools the "armor of God." We can use the Word of God to stand against the enemy and discern if our thoughts are right and true.

Discuss   Go through Ephesians 6 again and discuss each piece of the armor of God and what it represents.

Talk about the concept of the Word of God being living and active. (It is powerful and brings life to all who read and internalize it.)

Talk about a time when the Word of God "came alive" to you.

Beauty   Read "In the Secret of His Presence" by Ellen Lakshmi Goreh.
Recite any portions from memory or copy your favorite stanza.

Recite   Recite Philippians 4:6.

Pray   Thank God for the gift of the armor of God.

Invite God to discern your thoughts and intentions of your heart.

Ask God to help you love His word more.

Bible Notebook

Write a list of the pieces of the armor of God on the lines in your Bible Notebook. Draw a picture of you wearing real armor with all of the pieces. Label your drawing.

DAY 5

Declare   Say "I will take my thoughts captive and think on true things" three times.

Sing   Sing the hymn "Turn Your Eyes Upon Jesus" and follow along with the lyrics sheet.

Read   Read Isaiah 26:3 and 2 Timothy 1:7.

Fear is one of the most difficult things to control. When fear comes into our minds and hearts, remember that fear doesn't come from God. Fight those fearful thoughts and feelings by dwelling on the truth. We are promised peace from God when we choose to fix our minds on Him and trust Him.

Discuss   Talk about a time when you were very afraid. What was going on in your mind? How did you overcome that?

What are some ways you can overcome fear when it rushes in? (Examples: Deep breathing, prayer, playing worship music, reciting scripture.)

What is a sound mind?

Beauty   Replicate a portion or all of this week's artwork or draw or paint what you imagine when you read this week's poem.

Recite   Recite Philippians 4:6.

Pray   Thank God for offering us the gift of peace.

Tell God you trust Him with your fears.

Ask God to remind you to focus on Him in fearful moments.

Bible Notebook

Copy Isaiah 26:3 in your Bible Notebook and draw a picture of yourself. Add a thought bubble and write things inside that you could choose to think about when faced with fear.

Wisdom:
I will accept correction and guidance with humility.

Declaration: I will accept correction and guidance with humility.

Song: "Refiner's Fire"

Verse: Proverbs 12:15

Poem: "At My Redeemer's Feet" by Johnson Oatman, Jr.

Artwork: *Mary Magdalene at the Feet of Jesus* by James Tissot

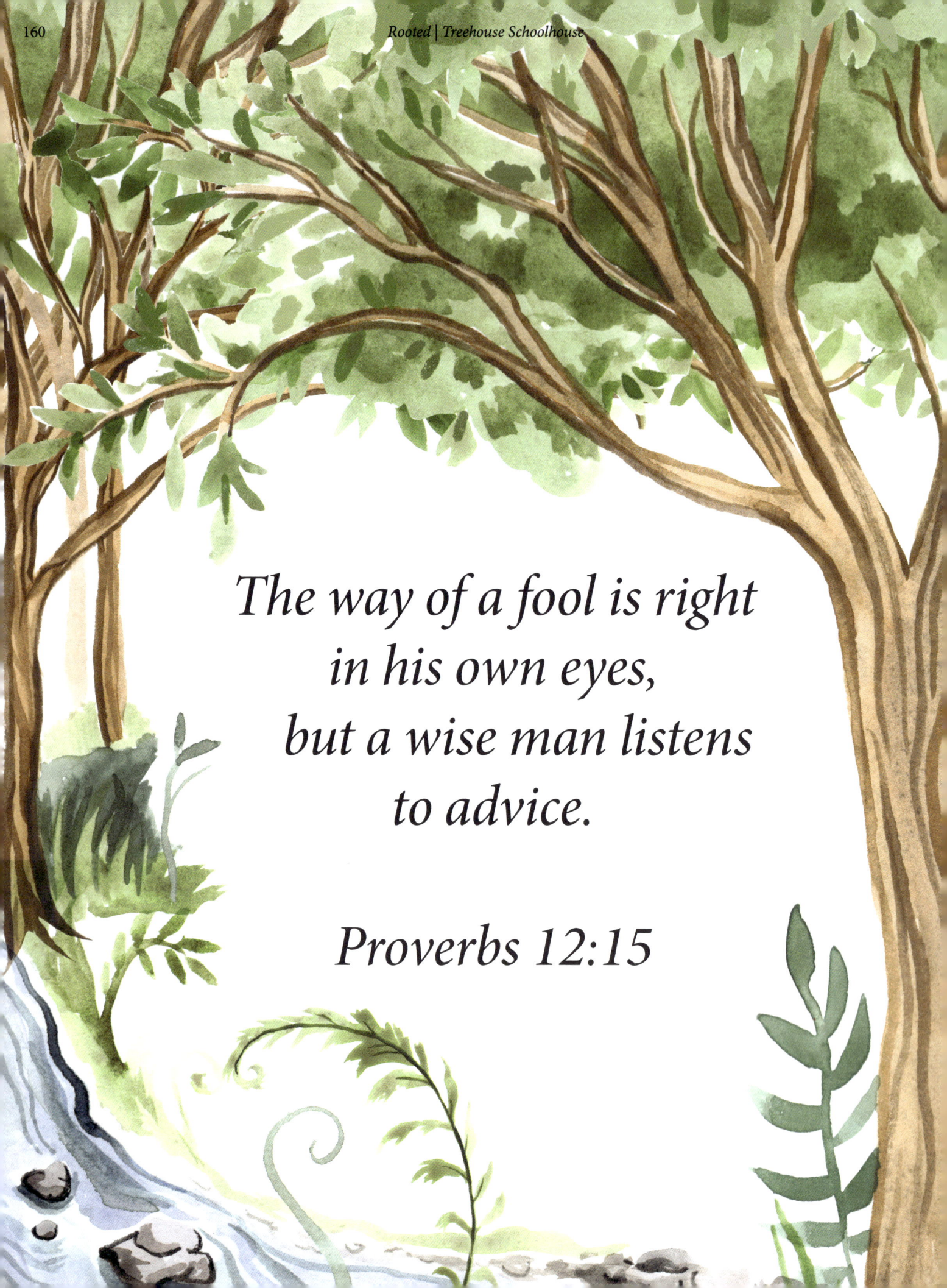

The way of a fool is right
in his own eyes,
but a wise man listens
to advice.

Proverbs 12:15

Wisdom: I will accept correction and guidance with humility.

Refiner's Fire

Purify my heart
Let me be as gold and precious silver
Purify my heart
Let me be as gold, pure gold

Refiner's fire
My heart's one desire
Is to be holy
Set apart for You, Lord
I choose to be holy
Set apart for you my Master
Ready to do Your will

Purify my heart
Cleanse me from within and make me holy
Purify my heart
Cleanse me from my sin, deep within

Refiner's fire
My heart's one desire
Is to be holy
Set apart for You, Lord
I choose to be holy
Set apart for you my Master
Ready to do Your will
(repeat)

And I am ready to do Your will
Make me ready to do Your will

I ask not for the highest place,
But find a spot more sweet
Where God bestows on me His grace—
At my Redeemer's feet.

Tho' waves of darkness round me roll,
I have a safe retreat;
No storm can ever harm a soul
At my Redeemer's feet.

He gives me from His loving hand
"The finest of the wheat."
I live in Heaven's borderland—
At my Redeemer's feet.

And when I reach the mystic sea,
Where earth and Heaven meet,
I'll spend a blest eternity
At my Redeemer's feet.

Come joy or pain, come weal or woe,
In Christ I am complete;
My highest place is lying low
At my Redeemer's feet.

"At My Redeemer's Feet"
by Johnson Oatman, Jr.

Wisdom: I will accept correction and guidance with humility.

Mary Magdalene at the Feet of Jesus by James Tissot
ca. 1886-1894

DAY 1

Declare — Say "I will accept correction and guidance with humility" three times.

Sing — Sing the hymn "Refiner's Fire" and follow along with the lyrics sheet.

Read — Read Proverbs 10:17, 12:1, 13:1, and 15:32.

The opposite of wisdom is foolishness. When we aren't humble and reject correction, we are choosing a foolish path that will ruin our lives. We are called to be an example of godliness by walking on the path of life.

Discuss — How do our choices between walking in wisdom or foolishness affect others?

Discuss what you know about the foolish man vs. the wise man from previous lessons and scriptures you have read.

Why do some people choose to walk in foolishness rather than wisdom?

Beauty — Observe *Mary Magdalene at the Feet of Jesus* by James Tissot.
Play Hide & Describe.

Recite — Recite Proverbs 12:15.

Pray — Tell God you want to walk on the path of life and wisdom.

Ask God to help you be a good example to others who are watching your choices in life.

Ask God to show you any specific areas in your life that need correction or guidance right now.

Bible Notebook

Using your Bible and what you have learned so far, contrast the wise and foolish man by writing two lists of characteristics and actions of each kind of person. Draw a picture to represent your lists. (Idea: Two paths or people that represent wisdom and foolishness.)

DAY 2

Declare Say "I will accept correction and guidance with humility" three times.

Sing Sing the hymn "Refiner's Fire" and follow along with the lyrics sheet.

Read Read 1 Peter 5:1-6 and Proverbs 11:14.

When God puts people in our lives to guide us with wisdom and correction, we must have humility in our hearts in order to receive it. Humility is recognizing that someone else may know more about something than we do. When we are humble, we are willing to receive correction, leadership, and wisdom from others without being arrogant or defensive.

Discuss Talk more about the meaning of the words "humility" and "humble" and what they look like in a person's life.

Share a story of a time you were given direction or wisdom from someone in your life. Did you heed it with humility? What was the outcome?

Refer back to the passage and talk about good leadership. What is God's charge to people in leadership roles?

Beauty Read "At My Redeemer's Feet" by Johnson Oatman, Jr.
Discuss any unknown vocabulary and meanings.

Recite Recite Proverbs 12:15.

Pray Thank God for the people in your life who offer you wisdom, correction, and guidance.

Ask God to forgive any areas of your heart that are arrogant towards correction and guidance.

Tell God you want to stay on the path of wisdom.

Dig Deeper

Use your Bible's reference pages or the internet to find more scripture on humility and pride. Locate a few in the Bible, then read and discuss. Copy one or more of the scriptures in your Bible Notebook and illustrate.

DAY 3

Declare Say "I will accept correction and guidance with humility" three times.

Sing Sing the hymn "Refiner's Fire" and follow along with the lyrics sheet.

Read Read Proverbs 16:1-3, 9, 18, and 25.

Willingness to accept wisdom from God is even more important than accepting wisdom from others. The Bible reminds us that while we think we know the right steps to take in our lives, God ultimately has the best path for us. We must come humbly to our heavenly Father and ask for wisdom and guidance in all situations throughout our lives and be willing to heed His wisdom.

Discuss Talk about a situation when you sought God's wisdom. How did you know what to do and what was the outcome?

Discuss how God speaks to us and what it may look like to "hear" and receive that wisdom. (Through the Bible, our hearts, and trusted people.)

What do these verses warn us about walking in arrogance and pride?

Beauty Observe *Mary Magdalene at the Feet of Jesus* by James Tissot.
What emotions do you think the woman in the picture feels?

Recite Recite Proverbs 12:15.

Pray Thank God for knowing the perfect path for your life and for being willing to guide you.

Ask for God's direction for something specific in your life right now.

Ask God to help you hear Him more clearly through His word and the Holy Spirit.

Role Play

Break into two teams and create short skits to perform. Choose a few situations and act out responding to correction in humility or pride.

DAY 4

Declare — Say "I will accept correction and guidance with humility" three times.

Sing — Sing the hymn "Refiner's Fire" and follow along with the lyrics sheet.

Read — Read Proverbs 3:5-6, Psalm 32:8-9, and Matthew 7:7-11.

We must admit that trying to figure out life on our own is foolish. Our Creator knows us best and knows what paths in life will bring us the most peace and joy, and fulfill His will for us on earth. It is our responsibility to seek God for guidance, receive it, and trust and obey.

Discuss — Talk about how guidance, discipline, and correction are God's gifts to us. Do you view this positively or negatively?

Why is trust so important in our relationship with God?

Talk about what Psalm 32:9 means. What is a bit and bridle?

Beauty — Read "At My Redeemer's Feet" by Johnson Oatman, Jr.
Recite any portions from memory or copy your favorite stanza.

Recite — Recite Proverbs 12:15.

Pray — Ask God for guidance in something specific in your life right now.

Tell God you trust Him with your life and the direction it takes.

Thank God for His good gifts of guidance, discipline, and correction.

Bible Notebook

Copy Psalm 32:8-9 or a portion of it. Draw a picture of a horse in the blank space. Include the bit and bridle and label them. Use books or the internet for inspiration.

DAY 5

Declare	Say "I will accept correction and guidance with humility" three times.
Sing	Sing the hymn "Refiner's Fire" and follow along with the lyrics sheet.
Read	Read Hebrews 12:1-11.

A good father corrects and disciplines his children out of a deep love for them. In the same way, God disciplines His children. It is up to us to humbly receive correction and guidance from God. Often discipline is uncomfortable, but when we choose to accept it, we come out on the other side with a more fruitful and abundant life.

Discuss   Imagine a world or life with no guidance or discipline from parents or God. What would that be like?

Tell a story of a time when you were corrected or disciplined and it felt painful or uncomfortable. What fruit was produced in the end?

What is at the heart of a parent or God disciplining their children? Why is it so important?

Beauty   Replicate a portion or all of this week's artwork or draw or paint what you imagine when you read this week's poem.

Recite   Recite Proverbs 12:15.

Pray   Humble yourself and tell God you want to receive His discipline and correction.

Ask God for forgiveness for times you have responded to Him or authorities with pride.

Thank God for being a loving Father, willing to guide and correct to keep you on the path of life.

Hymn / Nature Study

Talk about the hymn this week and what "refiner's fire" means. Scan the QR code in the introduction to watch the video about how silver is refined. Look up Zechariah 13:9, 1 Peter 1:7 and Malachi 3:2-3 and discuss.

Wisdom: I will be a good steward of all that I have.

Declaration: I will be a good steward of all that I have.

Hymn: "Take My Life and Let it Be"

Verse: Colossians 3:23-24

Poem: "Son of God, Eternal Savior" by Somerset Corry Lowry

Artwork: *The Widow's Mite* by James Tissot

Whatever you do, work heartily, as for the Lord and not for men, knowing that from the Lord you will receive the inheritance as your reward. You are serving the Lord Christ.

Colossians 3:23-24

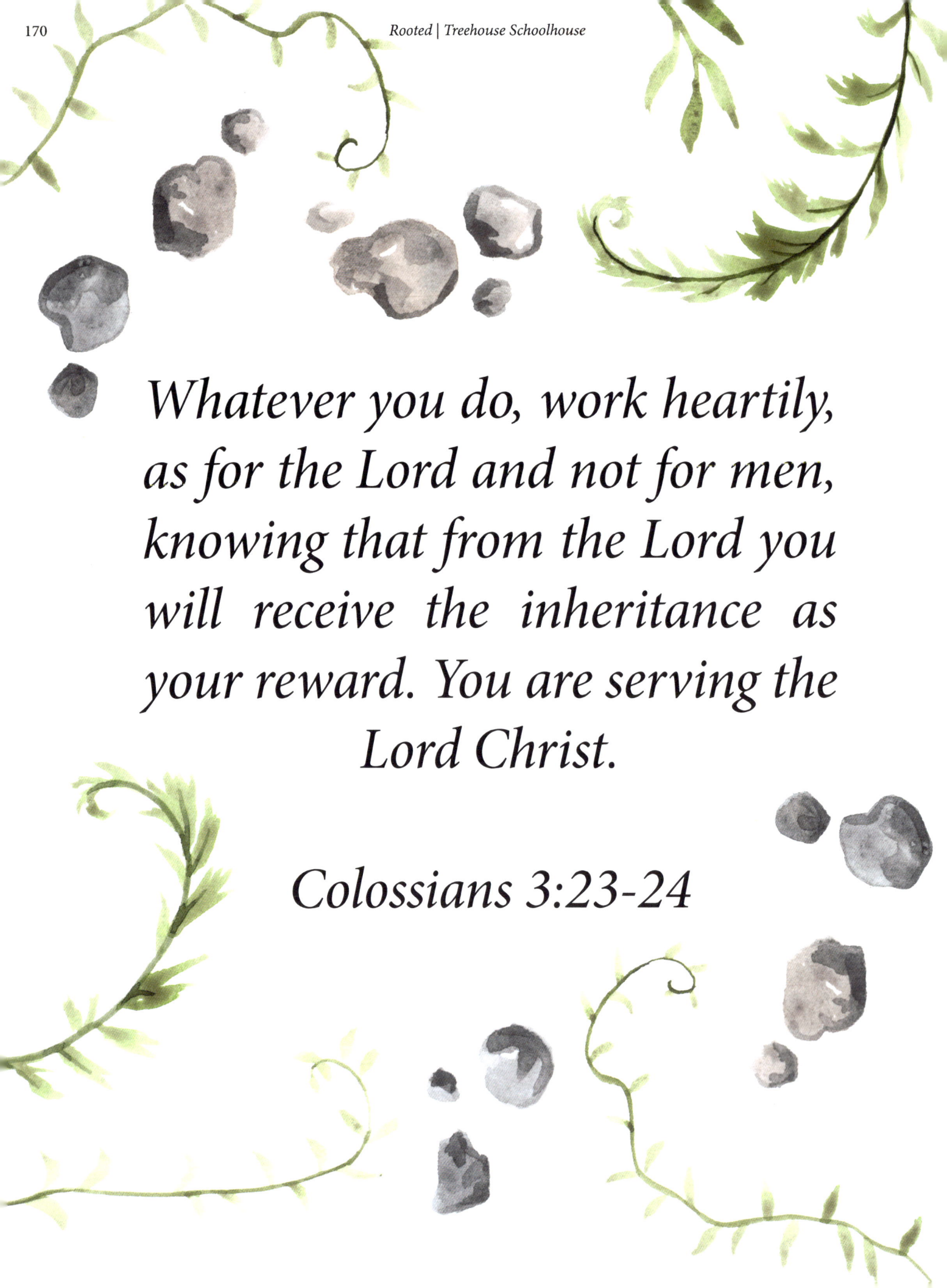

Take My Life and Let it Be

Take my life and let it be
Consecrated, Lord, to Thee
Take my hands and let them move
At the impulse of Thy love
At the impulse of Thy love

Take my feet and let them be
Swift and beautiful for Thee
Take my voice and let me sing
Always, only, for my King
Always, only, for my King

Take my lips and let them be
Filled with messages for Thee
Take my silver and my gold
Not a mite would I withhold
Not a mite would I withhold

Take my love; my God, I pour
at Thy feet its treasure store
Take myself and I will be
Ever, only, all for Thee
Ever, only, all for Thee

Take my life and let it be
Consecrated, Lord, to Thee
Take myself and I will be
Ever, only, all for Thee
Ever, only, all for Thee

Take myself and I will be
Ever, only, all for Thee
Ever, only, all for Thee

Son of God, eternal Savior,
source of life and truth and grace,
Word made flesh, whose birth among us,
hallows all our human race,
you our head, who, throned in glory,
for your own will ever plead:
fill us with your love and pity,
heal our wrongs and help our need.

As you, Lord, have lived for others,
so may we for others live.
Freely have your gifts been granted;
freely may your servants give.
Yours the gold and yours the silver,
yours the wealth of land and sea;
we but stewards of your bounty
held in solemn trust will be.

Son of God, eternal Savior,
source of life and truth and grace,
Word made flesh, whose birth among us
hallows all our human race,
by your praying, by your willing
that your people should be one,
grant, O grant our hope's fruition:
here on earth your will be done.

Exerpt from "Son of God, Eternal Savior"
by Somerset Corry Lowry

Wisdom: I will be a good steward of all that I have.

The Widow's Mite by James Tissot
ca. 1886-1894

DAY 1

Declare	Say "I will be a good steward of all that I have" three times.
Sing	Sing the hymn "Take My Life and Let it Be" and follow along with the lyrics sheet.
Read	Read 1 Chronicles 29:10-16 and James 1:17.
	Everything we have is a gift from God. Being a good steward means taking responsibility and caring for what we have. In David's prayer, he acknowledges that everything he offers as worship comes from God's hand. One way to worship God is to properly care for what He has given us and to give it all back to Him.
Discuss	What does it mean to give everything back to God?
	Talk about what God has given you as a family. Think beyond material possessions.
	Talk about the word steward. How can you be a good steward of what God has given you?
Beauty	Observe *The Widow's Mite* by James Tissot. Play Hide & Describe.
Recite	Recite Colossians 3:23-24.
Pray	Ask God to help you care for your things in a way that shows gratitude and good stewardship.
	Thank God for all He has given you. Be specific.
	Tell God you want to worship Him by offering it all back to Him.

Family Connection

Look around your home and choose a project to do together to practice good stewardship of what God has given you. Ideas: Organize a closet, clean the backyard, or clean out the refrigerator.

Wisdom: I will be a good steward of all that I have.

DAY 2

Declare — Say "I will be a good steward of all that I have" three times.

Sing — Sing the hymn "Take My Life and Let it Be" and follow along with the lyrics sheet.

Read — Read Matthew 15:14-30.

Just like in this parable, God has given each person a measure of material possessions, talents, and gifts. We are responsible for using them in a way that "multiplies" them and gives God glory. The promise in verse 29 is that when we are faithful with what we are given, He will give us more.

Discuss — What does it look like to be faithful with what God has given us?

How can we take what God has given us and invest or grow it? Think about this both in light of material possessions and your talents.

Talk about the gifts and talents that each member of your family has and how to use them for God's glory.

Beauty — Read "Son of God, Eternal Savior" by Somerset Corry Lowry.
Discuss any unknown vocabulary and meanings.

Recite — Recite Colossians 3:23-24.

Pray — Thank God for how He made you and tell Him you will use your gifts and talents for Him.

Ask God for clarity on how to multiply what He has given you.

Take turns praying for one another. Pray that God would use each member of your family for His glory.

Role Play

Act out the Parable of the Talents in Matthew 15 using some coins. Take turns being the various characters in the story. Refer to the passage if you need prompts on what to say and do.

DAY 3

Declare	Say "I will be a good steward of all that I have" three times.
Sing	Sing the hymn "Take My Life and Let it Be" and follow along with the lyrics sheet.
Read	Read 1 Peter 4:9-11.
	By God's grace, we have all been given gifts. When we serve others using these gifts with the right heart, we are serving God. This is worship to Him. Some of these gifts are material things and some are things you can't see.
Discuss	Talk about a time someone served you and you felt loved. What gifts do they have and how did they use them?
	List some material things you have that are gifts from God. List some unseen things that are unique to you.
	Discuss how you can serve others more as a family and make a plan or step to do that.
Beauty	Observe *The Widow's Mite* by James Tissot. What do you think the people in the background are thinking and saying?
Recite	Recite Colossians 3:23-24.
Pray	Ask God to forgive you for times you were selfish with your time, money, and talents.
	Ask God for help in serving others. Be specific in your prayer with who you want to serve and how.

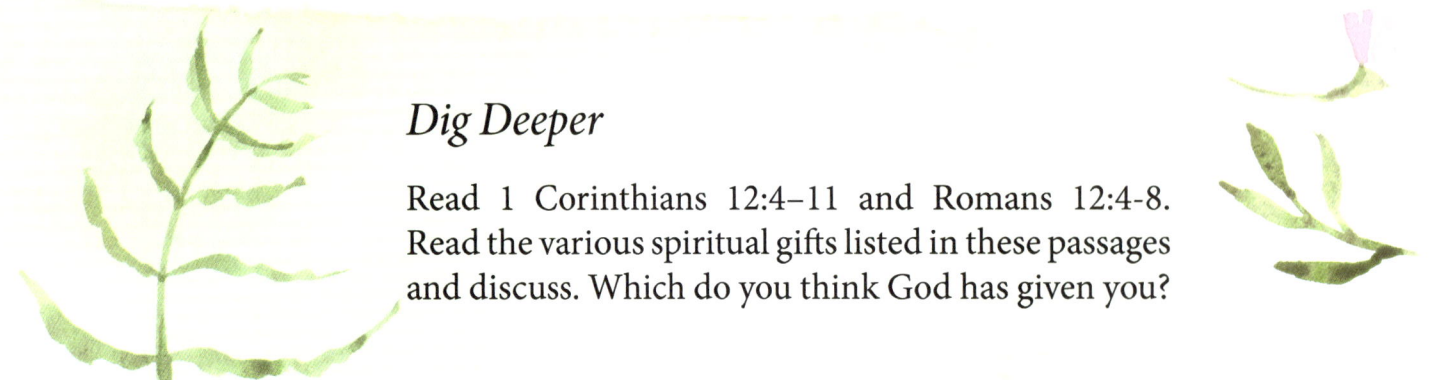

Dig Deeper

Read 1 Corinthians 12:4–11 and Romans 12:4-8. Read the various spiritual gifts listed in these passages and discuss. Which do you think God has given you?

Wisdom: I will be a good steward of all that I have.

DAY 4

Declare — Say "I will be a good steward of all that I have" three times.

Sing — Sing the hymn "Take My Life and Let it Be" and follow along with the lyrics sheet.

Read — Read Luke 16:10-13 and 1 Timothy 6:17-19.

As followers of Jesus, we are called to be good stewards of money. It starts with remembering that it all comes from God and our job is to use it well in our lifetime. When we put money in its proper place in our hearts, it can be a tool to further the kingdom. When money is not in its proper place, we can become a slave to it and it can pull us away from God.

Discuss — What are some ways you can be wise with your money?

Talk about the concepts of being faithful or dishonest with little and with much presented in Luke 16:10-12.

Talk about slavery. What does life look like for someone who is a slave to money?

Beauty — Read "Son of God, Eternal Savior" by Somerset Corry Lowry.
Recite any portions from memory or copy your favorite stanza.

Recite — Recite Colossians 3:23-24.

Pray — Thank God for your material possessions and money. Tell God it all belongs to Him.

Ask God to show you how to walk in wisdom with your finances.

Ask for forgiveness for times you have been selfish or have not been wise with your money.

Math

Do a hands-on math lesson using real or pretend money. Adapt it to your child's level by using addition, subtraction, multiplication, or division. Present a few story word problems that incorporate being a good steward of money.

DAY 5

Declare Say "I will be a good steward of all that I have" three times.

Sing Sing the hymn "Take My Life and Let it Be" and follow along with the lyrics sheet.

Read Read Mark 12:41-44.

The widow didn't have much, but she gave all she had. This gift pleased Jesus more than the rich people who gave large sums. Even if we don't have much to offer (time, money, or talents), when we give sacrificially, this pleases Him.

Discuss What areas of your life do you feel like you don't have much to give?

How can you give what you do have to the Lord? Think outside the box.

Talk about why we give money to churches and ministries and the work they do with the money.

Beauty Replicate a portion or all of this week's artwork or draw or paint what you imagine when you read this week's poem.

Recite Recite Colossians 3:23-24.

Pray Tell God that even in areas where you don't have much, you offer it freely to Him.

Ask God to show you how to use what you have (even if it's small) for Him.

Pray for your church and for the leadership to have wisdom on how to steward their finances well.

Bible Notebook

Write a summary of the story you read today and draw a picture to represent it.

Wisdom:
I will resist temptation and say no to sin.

Declaration: I will resist temptation and say no to sin.

Hymn: "Come Thou Fount"

Verse: Titus 2:11-12

Poem: "When You Suffer Satan's Temptings"

Artwork: *Jesus Tempted in the Wilderness* by James Tissot

For the grace of God has appeared, bringing salvation for all people, training us to renounce ungodliness and worldly passions, and to live self-controlled, upright, and godly lives in the present age.

Titus 2:11-12

Come Thou Fount

ome, thou Fount of every blessing
Tune my heart to sing Thy grace
Streams of mercy, never ceasing
Call for songs of loudest praise
Teach me some melodious sonnet
Sung by flaming tongues above
Praise the mount! I'm fixed upon it
Mount of thy redeeming love

Here I raise mine Ebenezer
Hither by thy help I've come
And I hope, by Thy good pleasure
Safely to arrive at home
Jesus sought me when a stranger
Wandering from the fold of God
He, to rescue me from danger
Interposed His precious blood

O to grace how great a debtor
Daily I'm constrained to be
Let thy goodness, like a fetter
Bind my wandering heart to Thee
Prone to wander, Lord, I feel it
Prone to leave the God I love
Here's my heart, O take and seal it
Seal it for Thy courts above
Prone to wander, Lord, I feel it
Prone to leave the God I love

When you suffer Satan's temptings,
Pow'rs of darkness gather 'round.
Devils urge you much to slacken,
That a crown may not abound.

Soldier, stand by grace empowered,
Mindful of th'ascended Lord.
Jesus surely conquered Satan;
Bravely wield the Spirit's sword.

Though your friends shrink back and tremble,
One with Satan silently,
Neighbors ridicule, reviling,
Siding with the enemy.

When the world shows ease and pleasure,
Sets for you a blissful net,
When you face vainglory's offer,
When you stumble, faith forget.

When the family's load is heavy,
Naught of natural strength avails,
Suffering losses inward, outward,
Even labor's profit fails.

Soon the battle will be over,
Satan's forces will be turned.
Soon the Church will hear the trumpet,
Glory and triumph is earned.

Now the King returns in triumph,
Rules the world by God's decree;
Now all nations bow before Him,
Praising Jesus reverently.

Exerpt from "When You Suffer Satan's Temptings"

Wisdom: I will resist temptation and say no to sin.

DAY 1

Declare Say "I will resist temptation and say no to sin" three times.

Sing Sing the hymn "Come Thou Fount" and follow along with the lyrics sheet.

Read Read James 1:12-15 and 1 Corinthians 10:13.

In this world, every person faces temptation. When we face temptation, we can remember that God's grace is with us, empowering us to say "no" to sin. We need to stop sin in its tracks when it is a faint desire and not allow it to grow like a weed that overtakes a garden.

Discuss What are the repercussions of living life in sin? Why is it so important to resist temptation?

Give examples of what temptation has felt like in your life and how you have resisted.

Talk about a time you have felt the lure of sin so strongly that it felt impossible to say "no." What happened?

Beauty Observe *Jesus Tempted in the Wilderness* by James Tissot.
Play Hide & Describe.

Recite Recite Titus 2:11-12.

Pray Thank God for the grace that He provides to say "no" to sin.

Ask God to help you resist a specific temptation you are struggling with.

Tell God you want to live a life of godliness and purity because you love and trust Him.

Role Play

Break into two teams and prepare a scenario where someone is tempted to sin. Role-play what they could do or say to resist the temptation. Perform your plays for the other team.

DAY 2

Declare — Say "I will resist temptation and say no to sin" three times.

Sing — Sing the hymn "Come Thou Fount" and follow along with the lyrics sheet.

Read — Read James 4:1-10.

We have a choice to make. Do we want to be friends with the world or friends with God? A life of wisdom is a life of saying "no" to sin and "yes" to God. To resist the devil and choose a life devoted to God, we need to walk in humility and lean into Him to give us the strength to choose His ways.

Discuss — Talk about why resisting sin is so important. Why does God have "rules" for our life?

Why does humility matter when it comes to resisting sin and living a life of wisdom?

What are some practical ways you can resist the devil? What does that look like?

Beauty — Read "When You Suffer Satan's Temptings."
Discuss any unknown vocabulary and meanings.

Recite — Recite Titus 2:11-12.

Pray — In humility, confess to God any sins you have been walking in.

Tell God what you will do to draw closer to Him.

Thank God for giving you the tools you need to resist the devil in moments of temptation.

Hymn Study

Watch a video about the history of the hymnist, Robert Robertson, by using the QR code in the introduction. Do some more research about his life on the internet.

DAY 3

Declare Say "I will resist temptation and say no to sin" three times.

Sing Sing the hymn "Come Thou Fount" and follow along with the lyrics sheet.

Read Read Matthew 4:1-11 and Hebrews 2:18.

Even though Jesus was tempted to sin, Jesus used the Word of God to combat the devil's temptations. One powerful way to prepare for temptation is to memorize scripture and recite it when sin is trying to lure us in. We can trust that Jesus understands the temptations we face and will help us.

Discuss Talk about how Satan is the great deceiver and how he used scripture to try to convince Jesus to sin.

How does it make you feel that Jesus understands what temptation feels like?

What are some scriptures you have memorized that would be helpful when you are tempted?

Beauty Observe *Jesus Tempted in the Wilderness* by James Tissot.
What emotions do you think Jesus is feeling as Satan is trying to tempt him?

Recite Recite Titus 2:11-12.

Pray Thank God for understanding you and what it's like to feel the weight of temptation.

Ask God to help you recall the truth when you are tempted.

Thank God for His Word.

DAY 4

Declare   Say "I will resist temptation and say no to sin" three times.

Sing   Sing the hymn "Come Thou Fount" and follow along with the lyrics sheet.

Read   Read Proverbs 4:23-27 and 5:1-14, 21-13.

This passage describes the repercussions of being lured off the path of wisdom by temptation. It also gives practical wisdom on how to keep your feet on the right path. In Proverbs 5, you can replace the woman with any sins that may lure you in and read it as an allegory.

Discuss   Define adultery, both in a spiritual and literal sense. Consider reading all of Proverbs 5 for children who are ready for more conversation on this topic.

Look through the passages and discuss what practical tips they give for staying on the path of life.

Talk about how sin can lead to both spiritual and literal death.

Beauty   Read "When You Suffer Satan's Temptings."
Recite any portions from memory or copy your favorite stanza.

Recite   Recite Titus 2:11-12.

Pray   Tell God how much you love Him and that you want to live a life that is faithful to Him.

Thank God for authorities in your life that guide you in wisdom.

Ask God to give you discernment when the things of the world try to tempt you.

Create

Draw or watercolor a heart. Cut it out and put it in an envelope addressed to God. Recall the line in this week's hymn: "Here's my heart, O take and seal it." Seal it with a sticker, tape, or a wax seal if you have one. Use it as a bookmark in your Bible.

DAY 5

Declare — Say "I will resist temptation and say no to sin" three times.

Sing — Sing the hymn "The Perfect Wisdom of Our God" and follow along with the lyrics sheet.

Read — Read Romans 12:1-2, Philippians 4:8-9 and 1 Peter 1:6-7.

Temptation always begins with a thought. As followers of Jesus, we are called to discipline our minds to think about good and godly things. The enemy is like a lion, looking for someone who will give in to temptation. When a tempting thought enters our minds, we must fight it immediately and cast it out.

Discuss — Discuss that having tempting thoughts isn't a sin, but what we do with them could be.

What temptations are you struggling with? Pinpoint how it starts with a thought.

How can you replace the tempting thoughts with something else?

Beauty — Replicate a portion or all of this week's artwork or draw or paint what you imagine when you read this week's poem.

Recite — Recite Titus 2:11-12.

Pray — Ask God to renew your mind with true and good thoughts.

Confess any ungodly or untrue thoughts you have allowed to linger in your mind lately.

Tell God you want to be a light in this dark world, rather than conforming to it.

Bible Notebook

Copy any verse or passage that stood out to you from the week's lessons and draw a picture to illustrate it.